Praying
God's Word
for Your
Husband

Praying
God's Word
for Your
Husband

Kathi Lipp

Revell

a division of Baker Publishing Group
Grand Rapids, Michigan

© 2012 by Kathi Lipp

Published by Revell
a division of Baker Publishing Group
P.O. Box 6287, Grand Rapids, MI 49516-6287
www.revellbooks.com

Printed in the United States of America

Library of Congress Cataloging-in-Publication Data
Lipp, Kathi, 1967–
    Praying God's word for your husband / Kathi Lipp.
      p. cm.
    Includes bibliographical references (p.) and index.
    ISBN 978-0-8007-2076-6 (pbk.)
    1. Wives—Religious life. 2. Prayer—Christianity. I. Title.
BV4528.15.L57 2012
248.3′208655—dc22   2012000772

The internet addresses, email addresses, and phone numbers in this book are accurate at the time of publication. They are provided as a resource. Baker Publishing Group does not endorse them or vouch for their content or permanence.

Published in association with the literary agency of WordServe Literary Group, Ltd., 10152 S. Knoll Circle, Highlands Ranch, CO 80130.

Prayer on page 140 taken from *When a Woman Inspires Her Husband*, © 2011 by Cindi McMenamin. Published by Harvest House Publishers, Eugene, Oregon 97402, www.harvesthousepublishers.com. Used by permission.

To protect the privacy of those who have shared their stories with the author, some details and names have been changed.

12   13   14   15   16   17   18   7 6 5 4 3 2 1

For my mother-in-law, Betty Dobson,

*who prayed for her husband every
day of their marriage.*

*And who prays for us
every day of our marriage.*

Contents

Contents

Acknowledgments

Linda Jenkins—I pray that God pours out his blessings on you in ways you would never expect . . . exactly how you have for me.

Justen the Guybrarian—Thanks for making me look a little smarter than I am.

Andrea Doering—I can't believe the series of chance meetings in the desert, canceled appointments, and taco lunches that led to this happening. Neither of us sought this book out, but God brought it all together as only he can. Thank you for showing up, being present, and letting me share my heart for husbands.

Rachelle Gardner—Andrea would never have known my name if it weren't for you. Thanks for always spreading good gossip about me, being brave when I'm not, and trusting in God and the process.

Sunnie Weber, Ginny Chapman, Lynette Furstenberg, Angela Bowen, Melodie Griffin, and Kimberly Hunter—a wise woman once told me, "You need as many people as you need to get you out the door to do God's work." Well, apparently I need all of you. Thank you for making it possible to do what God has called me to do. I love watching each of you work in your giftedness and in his plan.

I want to thank the women who poured out their hearts in prayer for their own husbands, as well as on behalf of husbands everywhere: Dineen Miller, Erin MacPherson, Michelle Koenig, Mimi Moseley, Emily Nelson, Cheri Gregory, Adelle Gabrielson, Cheryl Johnson, Carol Boyle, Robin Dilallo, Amy Redelsperger, Debbie Ruiz, Martha Orlando, Karen Jordan, Arlean Moses, Jane Jackson, Judy Parker, Karin McClay, Cindi McMenamin, Amy Cherry, Sarah Ward, Robin Patrick, Dawn Wilson, Melissa Krabbe, Vashie Miller, and Linda Carlblom. Thousands of men will be prayed for because of your honesty, transparency, and words.

Mom, Dad, Betty, the Richersons, and the Lipps—we are blessed to be surrounded by a family who loves unconditionally, gives unselfishly, and never, ever stops supporting us.

Amanda, Jeremy, Justen, and Kimberly—you keep life interesting and give me plenty to pray about. You are the joy of our lives.

Roger—it is a privilege to pray for a man as good as you. I love doing life with you and can't wait to see what God has in store for you next. (I have my verses all ready.)

Praying God's Word
A Husband's Perspective

by Roger Lipp

I don't know if I could pass a test to determine when my wife is praying for me and when she isn't. But I can say that it makes a huge difference knowing that she is praying. It changes my relationship with her. It changes how I see the world. It changes my relationship with God.

Without the prayer support from my wife, a bad day as an engineer at a high-tech company might look something like this:

8:00 a.m.: Start going through email at work. The computer servers in India aren't happy. People in India aren't happy because the servers aren't happy. Start trying to put the right solutions in place to make the servers happy again. But in the back of my mind, I'm feeling a little put-upon. This isn't how my day is supposed to start.

8:30 a.m.: Programs are crashing because of defects we introduced yesterday. More unhappy people. More solutions that need to be put in place. Still haven't finished with the servers. This isn't good timing. People are watching my project. Having these kinds of problems show up now will cost me. This isn't good. I'm a bit scared of what will happen.

9:00 a.m.: Unexpected meetings are scheduled to discuss problems that other unhappy people are having. My mood takes a turn for the worse. I have way too much going on to be sitting around in meetings discussing other people's problems. I know they aren't happy, but if I don't get out of here and start working on the other problems that have already come up in the day, I won't get anything done, and that would not reflect well on me. And in today's economy and job market, that's not a good thing. There seems to be a lot of unhappiness going around.

All this before I get my cup of coffee. Not a good day. But it happens. It's what I'm paid for. I can deal with it. But eventually I become, well, unhappy.

Now let's replay that day, this time going into it knowing that my wife is preparing my path with prayer.

8:00 a.m.: Unhappy servers.

8:30 a.m.: Crashing programs.

9:00 a.m.: Unexpected meetings. Unhappy people everywhere, just as before. But this time, I'm different.

I start to feel put-upon by the unexpected server problems in India. But instead of turning that into a woe-is-me moment, hold on . . . well, let's face it: I'm not really different, and it still becomes a woe-is-me moment. But after that, when I'm at home telling my wife about my day, she tells me that she's been praying for me. That gives me pause. I reflect on the various events of the day and see them now in retrospect, in a different light. Each presents an opportunity. Unhappy people need to be met with grace. A grace that I can give only out of a reservoir refilled by my Savior and the prayers of my loving wife.

Knowing that my day is covered in prayer—whether I'm having a good day or a bad day—changes how I can approach the next bad day. And there will be another one just around the corner.

In the midst of all that, there is a subtle change in my relationship with my wife. Through her specific prayers for me and my world, we are joined together in more intimate ways. She isn't a passive bystander in my life. She actively comes alongside in all things, even areas where she isn't directly involved. She becomes a loving partner in my struggles and a support in my weaknesses. I need that.

"The prayer of a righteous person is powerful and effective" (James 5:16). It's pretty easy for me to see the truth in that incredible verse. Not too long ago, I had been going through a bit of a dry spell. Getting anything done was painful, slow, and of dubious worth. I was getting rather concerned. Instead of a golden touch, I had something of a rust-and-tarnish touch. I felt out of sorts and muddled, and almost every day I had a hard time thinking clearly. I was becoming desperate and filled with self-doubt. What if there was something wrong with me? What if this wasn't just a temporary dip but a new way of life? How long could I keep my job? Would I be able to get another job? How would this impact my marriage? I was spiraling deeper and deeper into this pit.

One day, out of the blue, everything changed. My mind was clear. I was productive. I felt great. It was like a light switch had been turned on in my soul. It was exhilarating. That night I was sharing this with my wife, and she replied, "I'm so happy for you. I had been praying for this." I was honestly speechless for a moment. This was a dramatic turn of events. Prayer. Of course! Why didn't I think of that? She had been praying for me. I was getting deeper and deeper into my pit of self-doubt and despair, and she was praying for God to reach into that mess and pull me out. He did, and now I am reminded of God's amazing power and love reaching into the darkest shadows to bring new life.

I thank God each and every day for a wife who loves me enough to be a prayer warrior for me and my needs. I can walk through life with more confidence knowing she has my back in prayer.

As you are starting this prayer journey, be sure to pay attention to how God responds to your prayers. He may change your husband. He may change you. He may change your circumstances. Who knows what his response will be?

But know this: God is powerful, and your prayers are heard and answered.

PART 1

Preparing
for
Prayer

1

How to Use This Book

I'm excited that you have chosen to change your life—and the life of your husband—through prayer. I know you will identify with the hearts of the women who have shared with me their stories of hope and hurt, release and restoration when it comes to their husbands, themselves, and their marriages.

Many of the Scripture prayers were written and submitted by dozens of women across the country (and, in a couple of cases, outside the country). Each woman's husband and marriage are different, but they all have one thing in common: a deep desire to see God move in their marriage.

Whether you use this book on your own, in a group, or in an emergency is up to you. But I know from personal experience that you will see the greatest results if you pray for your husband in a variety of ways.

Everyday Prayer

One of the ways to use this book is in your everyday prayer time for your husband. No crisis, no emergency—just daily going to God and placing your husband in his hands.

Have a Time

It helps to have a consistent time each day for prayer. I used to pray in the evenings, when I was firing on all cylinders, but I soon realized I was trying to crowd more and more into my evenings and therefore praying (or not praying) later and later at night.

Now I pray first thing in the morning. Yes, I'm not always awake, and yes, there is a large amount of coffee involved. But in order to find a time that worked for me, I had to go through a whole bunch of times that didn't.

Even if you are not a morning person, give mornings a try, even if just for five minutes. It changes the way I live through my day. It helps me to live in an awareness of where God is already working and to move with an attitude of thankfulness.

You would think that with experiencing the results of daily prayer, I would be jumping out of bed to make it happen. Let me just say that this doesn't happen every day. I pray more than I did five years ago, but not as much as I would like to. But like every good habit in my life, prayer is a discipline that takes time to develop.

Have a Routine

Just as going to work, dropping your kids off at school, or going to your Tuesday morning kickboxing class becomes a routine in your life, so can praying for your man. Know that just committing to the priority of praying for your husband is more than most women will ever do. Everyone knows you are supposed to put time aside for personal development, but development for someone else? That is radical and countercultural.

So figure out a routine that works for you. You can pray through each chapter of the book in order, go straight to your biggest needs of the moment, or pick one prayer from each chapter for your prayer time. Or maybe you can use this book in a two-week format, every day praying through a "Prayers for Your Husband" chapter to make sure your husband is completely covered. Maybe there's a chapter of the book that needs your time and attention right now. That's okay. The fact that you are praying is amazing, brave, and wonderful.

Have a Spot

For most of the year, it's my kitchen table. During the summer, it's a chair on my back patio. For you, it may be a big overstuffed chair in the living room or the spot where you spend the most time—the driver's seat of your minivan or your desk at work. But having a spot is important.

Having a spot trains your mind to pray. When I sit at my kitchen table in the morning, my brain, after having had many years of training, goes immediately to prayer. (Well, to be honest with you, when my feet hit the kitchen floor, my brain—and those feet—go immediately to my Keurig one-cup coffeemaker. But eventually I make it to my chair and prayer.)

The other advantage here, even when I'm traveling and not at home, is that I can just imagine sitting in my lounge chair in the backyard, and every part of my body, mind, and spirit goes to that place of prayer. It's a powerful thing.

Have Some Stuff

Wherever your spot is, make sure you have a few things there that can lead you to prayer. Here is my list of stuff:

My Bible. I love *Maranatha! The NIV Worship Bible.* It's out of print, but you can still find plenty of used copies online.

A notebook.

A pen.

A book. I love that you are praying for your husband using this book. Here are some other books that have made my prayer and study time deeper and richer:

Jesus Calling: Enjoying Peace in His Presence by Sarah Young

Life of the Beloved: Spiritual Living in a Secular World by Henri J. M. Nouwen

Celebration of Discipline: The Path to Spiritual Growth by Richard J. Foster

A blanket. Even in California it can get cold in the winter!

I have all of these things in a corner of my kitchen so when I come downstairs in the morning, I am not fumbling around for my stuff.

Simple Prayer

Praying for your husband changes the way he walks through life. And for that reason alone, try to develop the habit of praying for him every single day. Even if it's in the front seat of your minivan, on a walk with your dog, or at your desk at work.

God is not looking for us to impress him with our prayers, but he does want us to be open to letting him impress our hearts. He delights in simple prayer. The Scriptures are filled with his people crying out to him in conversation, and he longs for us to be that personal with him. That is one reason Scripture prayer is so powerful. It's a cry out to God that doesn't have to be rehearsed or perfected—it's a reflection of God's own heart back to him.

That's why I have written out the Scripture as well as the prayer in later chapters. You may have a different approach to how to pray that particular Scripture. I want you to have the Scripture at your fingertips whenever you need it, but I also want you to have the freedom to pray in the way you see fit.

With a Small Group

Just last night I was praying with some other women who are leading an event I am part of. I was going to the meeting with kind of a hard heart. (That's the spiritual way of saying, "I don't wanna go!" and stomping my feet just a little.) I felt a bit resentful about giving up an evening when I could just as easily have prayed at home.

The reality was, however, I probably would not have prayed at home (I know that praying during commercials on the Home and Garden Network counts, but still . . .), and I would have missed out on some amazing opportunities to hear how other women were praying through their anxiety over getting everything done. I was better for having prayed and having been prayed for. It just took me getting off the couch to experience it.

I think the most powerful way you can use this book is with other wives—holding each other accountable to pray for your own husbands, and praying for each other's husbands.

Whether you are in the same Bible study group or you are praying by Skype with your sister in Denmark, you will find that you are more committed, are more consistent, and pray more confidently when you are praying with other like-minded women.

Maybe you commit to praying for two weeks between Bible studies, or the first two weeks of every month. Put it on your calendar, start with chapter 5, and pray through the "Prayers for Your Husband" chapters in two weeks. Keep connected by Facebook or email—whatever it takes for prayer to become a holy habit in your life.

During Challenging Times

Perhaps your man was just laid off from his job. Now not only is he unemployed, he may be feeling like he is no longer the man of the house—unable to provide for his family. Now he's around the house all day, snapping at you over the slightest infraction, real or imagined.

It's time to get very purposeful about your prayers. In a situation like this, I would run to certain chapters to find prayers that are more targeted: chapter 5 ("When He Feels Overwhelmed"), chapter 6 ("Employment"), chapter 8 ("When He Feels Inadequate"), or chapter 16 ("His Relationship with You").

Yes, there are many other chapters that would pertain to his situation, not to mention hundreds of verses. But when you feel overwhelmed yourself by trying to lift up your husband's burdens, keep it simple and pick a few verses to pray for him consistently.

Whatever the situation, now is the time to get pointed about your prayers, as well as seek out powerful Scriptures to pray.

In an Emergency

You got the middle-of-the-night phone call that no woman wants to get. Or there is some other crisis in your man's life. Grab this book as you are hitting your knees. An emergency is not the time to be hesitant about asking God for what you want. Dig out his promises in this book and pray them back to him.

And then don't be shy! When you are in an emergency, people want to help but don't know how. Give them the verses and the prayers to pray and then ask them—or beg them—to intercede on your behalf.

2

Preparing Your Heart to Pray for Your Husband

Maybe you picked up this book with your heart full of love and readiness to pray for your husband. Awesome!

But maybe you're a bit reluctant. Perhaps a friend suggested you read this book. Or maybe she wasn't that subtle. You may be telling yourself that you are just not in a place right now to be praying for your man. As I see and talk with wives around the country, one thing is clear—there are a lot of women who are resistant to praying for their husbands.

Several years ago, I spent three days at a conference with a woman who had a deep spirit of bitterness. It seemed like every sentence out of her mouth was about how one of her friends hadn't lived up to her expectations, how her boss was taking advantage of her, or how her kids didn't respond properly to the ways she was trying to show love to them.

And then there was her husband. There was not a thing he could do right. If he bought her flowers, they were the wrong ones. If he didn't buy her flowers, he was selfish and stingy. If he asked her what kind of flowers she wanted, she was ticked that he didn't already know. There was no way this guy could ever win. After spending three days with her, I wondered how she had anyone in her life at all.

While the spirit of this woman was a huge drain on everyone around her, the thing that made my heart break for her and the people in her life was that she was making no attempt to restore or repair those relationships. She was waiting for her husband to change. She was waiting for her kids to change. She was waiting for the people at church to change.

I was pretty sure she was going to be waiting a very long time.

Obstacles to Praying for Our Husbands

Now, I'm sure you're not as bad as that woman. But even as I judged her, there were things I could identify with. I can recognize a spirit of bitterness in others and myself, and there are many reasons a woman can become bitter or resistant to praying for her husband.

Being Forced into a Situation That Was Not of Your Own Making

Maybe before you got married, you and your husband made the decision that once kids came along, you would stay home and be a full-time mommy. But then your husband's job was cut back or cut altogether, and through no fault of yours, you needed to go back to work in order to keep food on the table. Unless you carefully guard your heart, it will be easy to become bitter in that situation. And most likely, that bitterness will be directed at your husband. We would all love to believe that with enough planning we can avoid any bad situation. But we can't predict all the problems that will come our way.

Unreasonable and Unmet Expectations

For a season, I got wrapped up in a silly and stupid "reality" show (the word "reality" is in quotes for a reason) about the fabulous lifestyles of some very fab women. They drove cars I'd never heard of, they lived in houses bigger than some of the churches I visit, and their shopping trips were things to be marveled at. One woman spent more on a pair of shoes than we spend on our mortgage.

I have to tell you, I started to turn just a wee bit green. Why didn't I have a life that was free from worry about money? Why did I have to clip coupons and budget for braces and play the "how long can I stretch between hair appointments" game?

I stopped watching the show because (1) it was a huge waste of time, (2) I would have been embarrassed if anyone knew I was watching it, and (3) I could see that I was starting to develop a spirit of bitterness. I was comparing my flea-market furniture that I thought was so charming with the designed-in-Milan pieces featured on the show, and I was starting to hate my stuff. I was comparing my husband's engineering job with their husbands' mogul-like enterprises. And he wasn't coming off so well.

Unforgiveness

Maybe your husband has done some things that hurt you. Maybe they're a little silly, or maybe they have really hurt you or those you love. The problem is, it's very hard to pray for someone when you haven't forgiven them.

Jealousy

Does your friend's husband bring her flowers on a regular basis or plan romantic trips for the two of them to go on—no kids allowed? Seems like a marriage made in heaven, doesn't it?

The reality? We are only invited onto the front porch of other people's relationships. Maybe their marriage is as good as it looks. But maybe not so much.

When our focus is on what others' husbands are doing for them and not on the husband God has given us, it's almost impossible to reach beyond ourselves and pray for the man sitting right in front of us.

Overcoming the Resistance to Prayer

When living with anyone for any amount of time, there are going to be grievances. Real "he did me wrong" kinds of grievances. I don't want to be cavalier about that. There are some deep hurts in marriage. But I do know this: as long as we are holding on to those wrongs like a balled-up tissue, we can never be truly free to hold out our hands in prayer on behalf of our husbands. This is brave stuff we're talking about here—giving up the right to be angry and getting on our knees instead of getting even. I long for the bitterness to stop—and at this point I'm talking about for your sake, not his. Scripture is very clear on how we are to handle bitterness:

> Pursue peace with all people, and holiness, without which no one will see the Lord: looking carefully lest anyone fall short of the grace of God; lest any root of bitterness springing up cause trouble, and by this many become defiled. (Heb. 12:14–15 NKJV)

As I read that verse, I got a very clear picture in my head of me kneeling in a garden, pulling up little shoots of bitterness. I want to be on my knees not just in prayer but actively pulling up those roots of bitterness. I don't want my bitterness to cause trouble, keeping me from doing the work—the prayer work—I'm appointed to do. And the hard part about those roots is that they have to be attended to all the time. I constantly need to be on my knees, praying to keep bitterness from growing out of control.

I get it—this prayer thing is some dangerous territory. But there is no better, safer place to be in your marriage than in constant conversation with your Maker. I hope you learn to love God better in the midst of your prayers, and from there the abundance of love and peace and justice you are experiencing spills out on your husband.

If your heart is resistant to praying for your husband, let me offer a few ideas of where to begin.

Ask a mentor or trusted friend to pray for you. Not several. You don't want this to descend into a gossip group. Just ask one other woman you trust to pray along with you.

Ask God to help you "want to want to." Right now you don't want to pray for your husband. So now is the time to ask God to help you want to pray.

Look for opportunities to pray. Maybe it's not about your husband. Maybe God is moving in other areas of your life right now that you need to pay attention to. Ask him to show up in your life in ways you don't expect. As you see miracles happening in other areas of your life or in the lives of the people around you, you will find it easier to believe in the miracle that can be your marriage.

3

Why Pray This Way?

When Roger and I were first married, I took a shooting-gallery approach to praying for him. I would go down a list of requests, praying over several areas of his life. I wanted to make sure I was doing everything I could to be the kind of wife God wanted me to be, as well as the kind of wife Roger needed me to be.

I worked hard to be faithful in my prayers for Roger. I would pray for every area of his life from parenting to work. I would pray almost every day in every way that I could think of.

And then I started to slip.

It felt like I was praying the same things over and over again without seeing any results. My prayer life had become stagnant, boring, and eventually close to nonexistent.

Not long after that point, we received a call from my brother-in-law Randy. Roger's mom was in the hospital. After some phone calls between California and Florida, Roger decided he would fly to the East Coast in a few days.

I knew that Roger was overwhelmed at work, was feeling guilty for being the only kid who still didn't live on the same coast as his mom, and was worried about her recovery. On top of that, he had been feeling run-down physically. I was very concerned for my husband.

Instantly it became so much easier to pray because I knew what Roger needed—strength. I prayed that he would stay strong physically—he already wasn't feeling well. I prayed that he would stay strong emotionally—it is so hard to deal with aging parents, especially when one is sick. I prayed that he would stay strong spiritually—I knew that in his exhaustion it would be easy to skip Bible study and being in the Word. I also knew that it was going to be hard for us to talk and for me to encourage him. I was traveling and speaking, and with a three-hour time difference, there were going to be a lot of challenges for us to stay connected.

As I spoke with Roger every day, sometimes for just a few minutes, I could hear how exhausted and overwhelmed he was. Roger loves his mom and hated to see her so weak. On top of his concern for her, he was also worried about our own kids and me.

I knew I needed to step up my prayers for my husband.

I started looking for Scriptures about strength that I could email to Roger, and for the first time I really thought about using those Scriptures as prayers.

When I found Psalm 46:1, "God is our refuge and strength, an ever-present help in trouble," I prayed, *Father, I pray that Roger would seek you as his refuge and strength. I pray that he would have knowledge of your presence and your help.*

And I kept praying. I prayed as I was on a plane to my speaking engagement in Oregon. I prayed as I was driving and when I went to sleep at night. I prayed as I made my coffee in the morning. I prayed because I knew God's promises and I wanted them for Roger.

In the past, I had prayed almost wistfully, with a lot of disclaimers: "If it be your will," and "I only want what you want, God." And those things are true. But what I realized I was doing was praying meekly so as not to put too many demands on God. Isn't that how most girls are raised, to not be too demanding?

This time it was different. I was praying Scripture, so I didn't have to wonder if it was God's will. I was praying the promises that God had set out in his Word. Praying Scripture over my husband gave me a new freedom in my petitions to God.

I have now incorporated Scripture into almost every part of my prayer life. When I'm faced with an issue, whether it's as mundane as praying for safety when we travel or as deep as wrestling with temptation, I'll find a Scripture that speaks to the issue and pray that verse.

I have found this invaluable in praying for Roger. When a need arises, I can find a verse that speaks to that need and pray for him.

It also makes my quiet-time reading more dynamic. When I'm reading through Scripture, I look at God's Word as actually applying to my life in a deeper way. Verses jump out at me as if God had only me in mind when writing those words.

As you look over these chapters and discover new ways to pray for your man, my prayer for you is that the benefits would not be just for him, but that you would experience a new level of depth and richness in your relationship with God. My prayer is that your conversations with the God who created you and loves you lavishly and deeply would take on the rhythm of two old friends talking, that there would be comfort, care, and love when you meet with him.

> Whatever I pray for my husband, from salvation to rest, I know my prayers are being answered and will continue to be. How? Psalm 37:4 says, "Delight yourself also in the Lord, and He shall give you the desires of your heart" (NKJV).
>
> *Karen*

It's hard for me to put into words how praying Scripture has changed me, my husband, and our family. I used to approach prayer as a checklist, something that had to be done in order for me to carry my "Good Girl Christian" card. Now prayer feels about as natural as breathing. Praying Scripture has caused three huge changes in my relationship with God and how I pray to him.

I Pray Boldly

Once I started praying God's own words back to him, I experienced a new way of interacting with my Creator. I was praying with a boldness I had never experienced before. I was unapologetic about how I was praying because I knew those prayers were from God himself.

> Then they came to Jericho. As Jesus and his disciples, together with a large crowd, were leaving the city, a blind man, Bartimaeus (which means "son of Timaeus"), was sitting by the roadside begging. When he heard that it was Jesus of Nazareth, he began to shout, "Jesus, Son of David, have mercy on me!"
>
> Many rebuked him and told him to be quiet, but he shouted all the more, "Son of David, have mercy on me!"
>
> Jesus stopped and said, "Call him."
>
> So they called to the blind man, "Cheer up! On your feet! He's calling you." Throwing his cloak aside, he jumped to his feet and came to Jesus.

"What do you want me to do for you?" Jesus asked him.

The blind man said, "Rabbi, I want to see."

"Go," said Jesus, "your faith has healed you." Immediately he received his sight and followed Jesus along the road. (Mark 10:46–52)

That is how I want to pray.

Bartimaeus asked boldly for what he wanted. First he called through the crowd. This was a pretty bold move for someone who was begging on the streets. And when he did come face-to-face with Jesus and was asked, "What do you want me to do for you?" he didn't hedge his bet—he didn't use qualifying language like, "If it be your will" or "If I'm not healed, help me accept that." Nope. It was out there—"This is what I want!" He ignored the doubters. He believed Jesus had the power to change things.

God's own Word makes it clear that what you ask for in his name, you will receive:

Therefore I tell you, *whatever you ask for* in prayer, believe that you have received it, and it will be yours. (Mark 11:24, emphasis mine)

Ask and it will be given to you; seek and you will find; knock and the door will be opened to you. (Matt. 7:7, emphasis mine)

Again, truly I tell you that if two of you on earth agree about anything they *ask* for, it will be done for them by my Father in heaven. (Matt. 18:19, emphasis mine)

And I will do *whatever you ask* in my name, so that the Father may be glorified in the Son. You may *ask me for anything* in my name, and I will do it. (John 14:13–14, emphasis mine)

If you remain in me and my words remain in you, *ask whatever you wish*, and it will be done for you. (John 15:7, emphasis mine)

This is the confidence we have in approaching God: that if *we ask anything according to his will*, he hears us. And if we know that he hears us—*whatever we ask*—we know that we have what we asked of him. (1 John 5:14–15, emphasis mine)

I Pray Continually

When I first began praying Scripture, I did pray about other areas of Roger's life, but that verse I had claimed for him (Ps. 46:1) was continually at the front of my mind. At times that verse of prayer became a meditation for me. I was able to roll it around in my brain and really ponder the Scripture.

Also, I had been accustomed to carrying around a prayer journal that I would pray out of. The problem? If I left my prayer journal at home, I was much less motivated to pray. My prayer time was like a formal, sit-down dinner instead of a relationship. I still write down the prayer requests I want to remember (and if I say I'm going to pray for you, I better write it down; otherwise I will have the best of intentions but no follow-through), but I needed to have a less formal way of staying connected to my Maker throughout the day.

I think about it like this. When Roger and I were first dating, our only time of talking deeply and really being connected was on a date—a scheduled time to be together. As our relationship grew, there were more times of connecting casually and easily—over a quick cup of coffee, a phone call, while running errands together. Even though our dating became less formal, our connectedness grew.

It has been the same in my relationship with God. When I first became a Christian at fifteen, my prayer life was pretty formal and planned out. I didn't know God very well, so there wasn't a lot of "hanging out" time. But as I grew to know him better, it became easier to integrate him into every part of my life.

Just as I still have dates with my husband (hey, that's one of the great benefits of being married: always having someone to take to the movies on a Friday night), I still need to have dates—time and intention set aside—with God.

Because it was only one verse I was praying (Ps. 46:1), it was easy to keep focused on it. I put an index card in my rental car with the verse written out on it. I highlighted the verse in my Bible and put a Post-it on my bathroom mirror. These were constant reminders to go to prayer on Roger's behalf. This was the first time in my life that I got a glimpse of what the instruction to "pray continually" (1 Thess. 5:17) really looked like.

I Pray Expectantly

As soon as all the people saw Jesus, they were overwhelmed with wonder and ran to greet him.

"What are you arguing with them about?" he asked.

A man in the crowd answered, "Teacher, I brought you my son, who is possessed by a spirit that has robbed him of speech. Whenever it seizes him, it throws him to the ground. He foams at the mouth, gnashes his teeth and becomes rigid. I asked your disciples to drive out the spirit, but they could not."

"You unbelieving generation," Jesus replied, "how long shall I stay with you? How long shall I put up with you? Bring the boy to me."

So they brought him. When the spirit saw Jesus, it immediately threw the boy into a convulsion. He fell to the ground and rolled around, foaming at the mouth.

Jesus asked the boy's father, "How long has he been like this?"

"From childhood," he answered. "It has often thrown him into fire or water to kill him. But if you can do anything, take pity on us and help us."

" 'If you can'?" said Jesus. "Everything is possible for one who believes."

Immediately the boy's father exclaimed, "I do believe; help me overcome my unbelief!"

When Jesus saw that a crowd was running to the scene, he rebuked the impure spirit. "You deaf and mute spirit," he said, "I command you, come out of him and never enter him again."

The spirit shrieked, convulsed him violently and came out. The boy looked so much like a corpse that many said, "He's dead." But Jesus took him by the hand and lifted him to his feet, and he stood up.

After Jesus had gone indoors, his disciples asked him privately, "Why couldn't we drive it out?"

He replied, "This kind can come out only by prayer." (Mark 9:15–29)

Because I was praying with a new boldness and passion, I waited expectantly for God's response. I stopped giving that silent shrug to heaven, feeling helpless about what was going on in Roger's life. While I didn't know how or when God was going to answer that Psalm 46 prayer, I knew it would be answered.

Also, it's a lot more fun to pray when you are praying God's Word. I don't feel like I'm going down a never-ending to-do list to make sure that Roger is covered. Instead I'm waiting to see what miracles God is working in my husband's life on a daily basis.

Waiting Expectantly When God Is Taking Too Long

I hate waiting. It's something I'm learning to do. But I hate learning to do it.

Last year for my birthday, my stepdaughter Amanda spearheaded the rest of our kids in getting me a Keurig coffeemaker. I am famous for not wanting to wait for an entire pot of coffee to be brewed before pouring myself a cup. In the wee hours of the morning, that can lead to spills, overflowing cups, and general mayhem. Plus I'm trying to cut down to one cup of coffee in the morning and a cup of decaf in the evening. So the kids thought that it was in everyone's best interest to get me a one-cup coffeemaker.

I was so excited to try out this little coffeemaker. No more waiting! Coffee instantly at the touch of a button.

Still, "instant" meant a full two minutes of waiting for the water to heat up and the coffee to steep. And for me, that's still too long.

I have a problem with waiting. I hate the feeling of getting nothing accomplished while I'm waiting. Two minutes doesn't seem like a lot of time to really get anything done, but it just feels like a waste of time.

That's why, when I'm told I need to wait on God, my coffee-honed instincts kick in and I rebel. I don't want to wait. I want things to change—and now. Waiting seems so passive, and being passive makes me crazy.

Recently, Roger and I had the privilege of worshiping at River Oak Grace Church in Oakdale, California. We listened to Pastor Paul Weissenborn talk about the "waiting verse," Isaiah 40:31:

Yet those who wait for the Lord
Will gain new strength;
They will mount up with wings like eagles,
They will run and not get tired,
They will walk and not become weary. (NASB)

He gave some insight into the verse that I had never heard before. He said the word *wait* used in this verse is the Hebrew word *qavah*. The literal meaning of the word is "to bind together like a cord." Pastor Paul explained that waiting as described in this verse is not a passive activity. Rather, as we bind ourselves closely to God—as some commentaries put it, we're bound together like strands of a cord or a rope—he will give us strength. Yes, we have to wait on him, but while we wait we are also growing deeper in and closer to him. We get so enmeshed in our Father that it becomes indistinguishable where our will ends and his begins. Awesome.

In this whole praying for our husbands thing, we have to learn to wait well.

Those are the reasons I now love praying God's Word back to him. It's a different way to pray for sure, but one that has the potential to change your life and your husband's.

4

Praying for Your Husband When He Doesn't Know God

You may be tempted to skip over this chapter if your husband walks with God, but I would encourage you to keep reading it.

Let me start off by saying that I'm married to a man who loves God and committed his life to Christ as a teen, so I have no real-life experience with being married to someone who doesn't believe as I do. But I have tasted the pain of knowing that some of my closest friends and dearest family members don't know Jesus. I can only imagine the hurt and fear that you feel because your husband doesn't know God. I do know that there have been times in Roger's life when other things crowded out his relationship with God. Work, kids, and even church activities took the place of a meaningful and daily communion with his Father. In these times, even though he was a believer, he was distant from God.

Two of my friends, Dineen Miller and Lynn Donovan, have written an excellent book called *Winning Him Without Words: 10 Keys to Thriving in Your Spiritually Mismatched Marriage.* I've asked Dineen to share how she prays for her husband, who isn't a believer.

When Your Husband Doesn't Believe

Praying for our husbands is the greatest gift we can give them, but it can also be our greatest challenge if they aren't believers. How do I know this? My husband and I have been married for almost twenty-four years as I write this, and sixteen of them have been as a spiritually mismatched couple. I am a believer in Jesus and my husband is an atheist.

In the years that I've prayed for my husband's salvation, there came a unique day in which God impressed upon me the idea that I should pray for my husband as if he were already a believer. A realization dawned in my heart and mind that my guy needed more than just prayers for his salvation. And why shouldn't I pray for all areas of his life? God can whisper in the ears of even the staunchest nonbelievers and use the circumstances of their lives to bring revelation. Look at the story of Balaam in Numbers 22. This man was a pagan prophet, yet God still used him in his plans for Israel.

And for those of you whose husbands once embraced a faith in Jesus, take heart in the story of Peter, who denied he knew Jesus three times and walked away (Mark 14:66–72), most likely ashamed of his failure and confused about how the kingdom of God would come with the death of their Messiah. Yet Jesus restored him three times, symbolically redeeming Peter's three denials (see John 21:15–19). Your greatest challenge will be to wait patiently as you pray for your husband's return to faith and to trust that Jesus is pursuing him with the goal of restoration.

Remember, just because our husbands do not embrace our faith in Jesus Christ and claim it as their own doesn't mean that God can't work in their lives on a daily basis. Our prayers for these men are vital to their future as well as our own.

With this new understanding, I strategically pray for my husband in four key areas. And I can think of no better way than using Scripture. God says his Word doesn't return void, so why not use it (see Isa. 55:11)?

Praying God's Word for His Salvation

Yes, this is a no-brainer and the most important area, of course. But sometimes in the waiting we lose our passion and focus as we pray. I love taking Scripture and putting my husband's name (or any loved one, for that matter) right into the verse and praying it aloud. Here are some passages you can pray for your husband's pending salvation.

And Elisha prayed, "Open his eyes, LORD, so that he may see." Then the LORD opened the servant's eyes, and he looked and saw the hills full of horses and chariots of fire all around Elisha. (2 Kings 6:17)

Lord, open my husband's eyes so that he may see you.

He has made everything beautiful in its time. He has also set eternity in the human heart; yet no one can fathom what God has done from beginning to end. (Eccles. 3:11)

Lord, you make everything beautiful in its time, and I know you are doing that in my husband's heart and life. You have set eternity in our hearts, and I ask that you awaken a yearning for your eternity in my husband's heart.

Jesus answered, "I am the way and the truth and the life. No one comes to the Father except through me." (John 14:6)

Jesus, reveal to my husband that you are the way and the truth and the life. Don't let him be confused by other religions and beliefs. Firmly set into his mind and heart that the only way to you, Father, is through your Son, Jesus Christ.

I keep asking that the God of our Lord Jesus Christ, the glorious Father, may give you the Spirit of wisdom and revelation, so that you may know him better. I pray that the eyes of your heart may be enlightened in order that you may know the hope to which he has called you, the riches of his glorious inheritance in his holy people, and his incomparably great power for us who believe. That power is the same as the mighty strength. (Eph. 1:17–19)

I keep asking that the God of our Lord Jesus Christ, the glorious Father, may give you, my husband, the Spirit of wisdom and revelation, so that you may know him better. I pray also that the eyes of your heart may be enlightened in order that you may know the hope to which God has called you, the riches of his glorious inheritance in the saints, and his incomparably great power for us who believe.

Praying God's Word for His Protection

Our greatest battle in this world will always be with the enemy, who is determined to discredit believers and keep the unsaved in his clutches. As wives of these dear ones, we are on the front lines, waging war for our husbands' souls. We play a vital part in God's plan for our unsaved husbands. And praying for their protection physically, mentally, emotionally, and spiritually is part of our roles as missionaries in our own homes. These will be some of the most powerful prayers you will speak into your husband's life. Each day as he walks out the door, pray for his protection.

I have given them your word and the world has hated them, for they are not of the world any more than I am of the world. My prayer is not that you take them out of the world but that you protect them from the evil one. (John 17:14–15)

Lord Jesus, as you prayed for your disciples' protection from the evil one, I ask for your protection for my husband from the enemy and his plans to hurt him or hinder his desire to know you in any way. And in your name, Lord, place your hedge of protection around my husband and keep him safe in your presence.

The god of this age has blinded the minds of unbelievers, so that they cannot see the light of the gospel that displays the glory of Christ, who is the image of God. (2 Cor. 4:4)

In the name of Jesus and his shed blood, I bind the god of this age and his minions from the mind of my unbelieving husband. No longer will my husband be blind to the glory of Christ. Jesus, reveal your image, your presence, your love, and your redemption to my husband.

But the Lord is faithful, and he will strengthen you and protect you from the evil one. (2 Thess. 3:3)

Lord, you are so faithful. I ask that you would strengthen and protect my husband from the evil one. Protect his mind, body, and soul from any plans the enemy has designed to tear him down.

Praying God's Word for His Role as Husband and Father

Oftentimes the lines of leadership can blur in a spiritually mismatched marriage. Though an unbelieving husband is unable to be the spiritual leader of the family (that role falls on the wife while he remains unsaved), he is still the leader of the family and needs prayer support for the roles he fills as husband and father. I encourage you to carefully read Ephesians 5:21–33. Study these verses and ask God to show you how to pray more specifically for your husband.

Husbands, love your wives, just as Christ loved the church and gave himself up for her. . . . In this same way, husbands ought to love their wives as their own bodies. He who loves his wife loves himself. (Eph. 5:25, 28)

Lord Jesus, help my husband to love me as you call all husbands to love their wives. Help him to see that we are better together, working in unity under Christ, to care for each other and our children.

Show me your ways, LORD,
    teach me your paths.
Guide me in your truth and teach me,
    for you are God my Savior,
    and my hope is in you all day long. (Ps. 25:4–5)

Lord, show my husband your ways and teach him your paths so that he can be a good husband and father. Guide my husband in your truth and teach him, for I know you desire to be his God and Savior.

He must manage his own family well and see that his children obey him, and he must do so in a manner worthy of full respect. (1 Tim. 3:4)

Lord, guide my husband in managing his family and inspiring his children with a daily role model that will instill respect for him. Bring godly men into his life. Show him what a godly man looks like and put a deep desire in his heart to be that kind of man.

Fathers, do not exasperate your children; instead, bring them up in the training and instruction of the Lord. (Eph. 6:4)

Father God, help my husband to be a good father to his children as you are a good, kind, and wise Father to your children.

Praying God's Word for His Role as Provider (and for His Workplace)

Sometimes I try to imagine the burden my husband feels to make sure we have enough money each day, week, and month to pay the bills, pay for food, and take care of the unexpected needs that inevitably crop up. Then add to the mix college tuition, medical expenses, and planning for retirement, and my guy may be feeling the pressure deeper than I realize. I couldn't have met those demands unless I knew two things: one, I was working to do what God had called me to do, and two, I knew people were praying for me.

Our husbands have neither reassurance because they aren't able to discern God's will for themselves yet, and they may not even like it when we tell them we're praying for them. Don't take it personally. Just understand that they don't see the need or believe it's pointless to pray to a nonexistent God.

I find in most cases, the more a husband protests, the more God is actually working in his life to dispel the lies and deceit the enemy has placed there. So join God in this ongoing work in your husband and cover him in prayers, asking God to help him be a good provider. Pray for his workplace, his attitude toward money, and wisdom to make good financial decisions. Here are some great Scriptures to get you started.

> The integrity of the upright guides them,
>   but the unfaithful are destroyed by their duplicity. (Prov. 11:3)

Lord, help my husband to be a man of integrity. Put godly men around him to model what that looks like. Steer him away from compromising choices, and when he's faced with one, give him the wisdom he needs to make the right decision.

> Do not store up for yourselves treasures on earth, where moths and vermin destroy, and where thieves break in and steal. But store up for yourselves treasures in heaven, where moths and vermin do not destroy, and where thieves do not break in and steal. For where your treasure is, there your heart will be also. (Matt. 6:19–21)

Lord, I pray that you would help my husband to be a wise steward of our money. Don't let him become so driven and consumed with money that he forgets who and what he is working for. Help him keep his priorities straight, and remind him continuously that his true treasure is at home with his family. And prepare his heart for you, Jesus, for you are the greatest treasure of all.

How, then, can they call on the one they have not believed in? And how can they believe in the one of whom they have not heard? And how can they hear without someone preaching to them? (Rom. 10:14)

Lord, you are near my husband in so many ways, working to bring him to belief. I pray that everywhere he goes in his workday, he'd see and hear people living out their faith in the workplace.

Praying God's Word for Yourself

Perhaps this is where the chapter should have started—with you. Ironically, as you grow, pray, and trust God more for the salvation of your husband and your marriage, you will be the one changed the most. Things you thought would never be possible will be. Things you thought you'd never accept, let alone praise God for, you will. Things you imagined and hoped for will arrive in ways you never imagined.

God loves to wow us. He loves to show us how much he loves us. Walking the path with an unequally yoked spouse is not easy. But I will tell you the greatest truth you will ever know in this journey.

You are not alone.

God has a plan and a divine purpose for you in your marriage. He's calling you to work and pray in ways you probably hadn't thought of. Most of them will be without a word, because in mismatched marriages, our actions speak the loudest. As daunting as that may sound, it's a journey full of grace and blessings. I promise you that. You hold a special place in God's plan—to be a sacred influence in your husband's walk toward faith. You are also on the front lines of battle. Just remember that truth I shared—you are not alone. Trust God with everything, and then prepare to see your life and marriage transformed in ways you hadn't even dared to dream.

As you pray for your husband, don't be afraid to pray boldly for yourself as well. You'll need to. You will also need others praying for you, so ask some trusted friends to uplift you in prayer—to be a prayer team for you. A soldier doesn't go into battle alone, so neither should you. And one of our greatest pieces of armor (Eph. 6) is our sword. Ladies, these Scriptures and prayers are just for you.

> But those who hope in the LORD
> > will renew their strength.
> They will soar on wings like eagles;
> > they will run and not grow weary,
> > they will walk and not be faint. (Isa. 40:31)

Lord, I place my hope in you. Renew my strength. When I grow weary, remind me to refocus my thoughts and hope in you because they've shifted to my circumstances. With you, Lord Jesus, I know I will not only persevere but also have joy in each and every day. Thank you!

> However, each one of you also must love his wife as he loves himself, and the wife must respect her husband. (Eph. 5:33)

Precious Lord, reveal to me areas where I am not respecting my husband. Show me how I can change so that my words and actions will affirm my husband and not tear him down. Help me to be the wife you desire me to be.

And we know that in all things God works for the good of those who love him, who have been called according to his purpose. (Rom. 8:28)

Father God, thank you so much for working for my good. Thank you for using all the circumstances in my life—good and bad—to strengthen my faith and to bring me closer to you. Lord, you are not only the redeemer of our lives but also the redeemer of our circumstances. I praise you for every victory and give you all the glory.

But thanks be to God, who always leads us as captives in Christ's triumphal procession and uses us to spread the aroma of the knowledge of him everywhere. For we are to God the pleasing aroma of Christ among those who are being saved and those who are perishing. To the one we are an aroma that brings death; to the other, an aroma that brings life. And who is equal to such a task? (2 Cor. 2:14–16)

Lord, help me to be the aroma of Christ in my husband's life. Where I am "stinky," help me to change. Fragrance my words and actions, Lord Jesus, so that my husband catches glimpses of you through me.

But he said to me, "My grace is sufficient for you, for my power is made perfect in weakness." Therefore I will boast all the more gladly about my weaknesses, so that Christ's power may rest on me. (2 Cor. 12:9)

Lord, help me to rely on your strength and allow you to work through my weaknesses to make me stronger. Use those places of growth in me to reach my husband as well. Help me to live my faith authentically so that my actions will be a loud testimony to my husband of your saving grace.

For the Spirit God gave us does not make us timid, but gives us power, love and self-discipline. (2 Tim. 1:7)

Thank you, Lord, that you did not give me a fearful spirit but one steeped in your power, your love, and a sound mind. Help me to remember this truth whenever I am afraid, overwhelmed, or losing hope.

And now here is my prayer for you, dear one. Put your name in place of each "you." Be blessed!

May the God of hope fill you with all joy and peace as you trust in him, so that you may overflow with hope by the power of the Holy Spirit. (Rom. 15:13)

PART 2

Prayers

for Your

Husband

5

When He Feels Overwhelmed

We can do nothing, we say sometimes, we can only pray. That, we feel, is a terribly precarious second best. So long as we can fuss and work and rush about, so long as we can lend a hand, we have some hope, but if we have to fall back upon God, ah, then things must be critical indeed!

A. J. Gossip

Your husband reminds you of Eeyore. There is a little black rain cloud following him everywhere he goes. He becomes moody and withdrawn and is looking to pick a fight about anything from the way you drive to the strength of the coffee you brew in the morning. Your man is overwhelmed.

Most likely, he's never going to say, "I feel overwhelmed with life." You're going to figure it out when he stops talking to you and retreats into his computer, the TV, or the garage. Or when he starts snapping at the dog for yawning too loudly.

It can be stressful and confusing for a woman when her husband is overwhelmed, for a couple of reasons: (1) what overwhelms men is very different from what overwhelms women, and (2) men don't usually share when they are feeling overwhelmed.

It's when my husband is the most overwhelmed that I feel the most helpless. I want to take action. I want to give him advice and do what I can to relieve the pressure.

There are plenty of things I can do. But by far, the most important thing I can do for him is pray.

Here are some reasons your man may feel overwhelmed and how you can pray for him.

Overwhelmed by the Big Stuff

It's the big stuff, compounded by all the little stuff, that can make our men feel stressed.

There is a lot involved in making sure that their families are provided for and protected. And sometimes that can be just plain overwhelming.

The definition of *overwhelm* is "to cover over completely, as by a great wave; to submerge; to overpower or crush." I would have to say that for the most part, my husband pretty much keeps his head above water. However, when he does feel tense, that description fits him perfectly. He's "covered over completely." He can lose sight of the hope he has in Jesus and see only the immediacy of his situation.

God is not surprised that we become anxious, but many men feel as if they have to soldier on—continually weighed down by the burdens of parenting, finances, work, and marriage—until at some point they can't stand under the pressure anymore.

Praying God's Word about the Big Stuff That Overwhelms Him

Ask me and I will tell you remarkable secrets you do not know about things to come. (Jer. 33:3 NLT)

Lord, you tell us that if we call on your name, you will answer. Help my husband to know he is not responsible for the weight of the world; you are. Allow him to come to the end of himself in a humble way so he will call out to you. Surprise him with what you have in store for him. Move in his heart to invite you to partner with him so he doesn't feel so alone.

The LORD is my light and my salvation—
   whom shall I fear?
The Lord is the stronghold of my life—
   of whom shall I be afraid? (Ps. 27:1)

Don't allow my husband to walk around in fear. I pray that he would see you as his support, his stronghold, and walk in confidence because of that.

But the Advocate, the Holy Spirit, whom the Father will send in my name, will teach you all things and will remind you of everything I have said to you. Peace I leave with you; my peace I give you. I do not give to you as the world gives. Do not let your hearts be troubled and do not be afraid. (John 14:26–27)

I pray my husband would know your peace and feel it. Lord, I pray that he looks not to the world for answers but to you. I pray that he would not be consumed with fear and anxiety but that he would have an untroubled heart.

For I am the LORD your God
   who takes hold of your right hand
and says to you, Do not fear;
   I will help you. (Isa. 41:13)

Thank you that you are who you say you are, and you are fully in control of all circumstances. Please let my husband feel your presence and comfort today in a tangible way. Thank you for the way you promise to lovingly come alongside him when he is overwhelmed. Please help him trade worry and fear for peace and complete trust in you. Let him find rest in the fact that you promise to help him with whatever is overwhelming him.

Work

I will never truly understand what Roger does for a living, but I do know the stresses he carries with him. Pleasing his boss locally and managing his teams both here in the States and overseas in India is a daunting task. Sometimes, with all the technology available to him and his company, it seems as if he is never off the clock.

And so I pray.

I pray for his value and worth in his job. I pray for his bosses and his co-workers. I pray that he has a job in the coming days. And I pray that all who encounter him will know whom he truly works for.

Praying God's Word When He Is Overwhelmed at Work

Be strong and courageous. Do not be afraid or terrified because of them, for the LORD your God goes with you; he will never leave you nor forsake you. (Deut. 31:6)

Lord, I know you go with my husband as he does his work. You will never abandon him. He is feeling overwhelmed today with the stress of life. Calm his fears and give him strength and courage to face anything that comes his way. Let him know you are holding him up so that he may persevere.

He says, "Be still, and know that I am God;
    I will be exalted among the nations,
    I will be exalted in the earth." (Ps. 46:10)

I pray that my husband can cease striving and know that you are the God of his life. I pray that he would put you in the proper place in his life.

From the ends of the earth I call to you,
    I call as my heart grows faint;
    lead me to the rock that is higher than I.
For you have been my refuge,
    a strong tower against the foe.
I long to dwell in your tent forever
    and take refuge in the shelter of your wings. (Ps. 61:2–4)

I believe your Word, which tells us that you love us. I know you see my husband's heavy heart right now. I know you are the answer for his every need. I ask you now to be his safe refuge, his fortress of strength. Protect his heart from the enemy. Encourage him and give him rest. He needs you now, Lord, and I know that you will lead him to rest in you. Thank you, Lord. Thank you, Jesus. Thank you, Spirit.

Family

There is a lot of controversy, especially in Christian circles, about the roles of men and women in marriage. But I have noticed a few things over the years of working with couples that seem to be pretty universal. One is that an emotionally healthy husband has a deep desire to do two things for his family: provide and protect.

Men take their role as provider seriously. And they know that a big part of their job is to keep their families safe—to make sure bad stuff doesn't happen to them. They think about everything from keeping the car safe to making sure the doors are locked at night.

Praying God's Word When He Is Overwhelmed about Family

Peace I leave with you; my peace I give you. I do not give to you as the world gives. Do not let your hearts be troubled and do not be afraid. (John 14:27)

I am praying today that you fill my husband with peace, that he will have a calm spirit instead of a frustrated spirit. I also pray for a peaceful evening here at home, that all the frustration and unfulfilled expectations will be removed from our family. Fill us with peace that surrounds each of us.

For he will command his angels concerning you
     to guard you in all your ways. (Ps. 91:11)

I am asking today, Lord, for protection for my husband and our whole family. Place your angels around every one of us throughout the day and night. Guard our thoughts and help each of us to walk down the right path. Help my husband to relinquish his fears for the family so he will not be overwhelmed.

Finances

A study by Jeffrey Dew at Utah State University finds that couples who reported disagreeing about finances once a week were over 30 percent more likely to get divorced than couples who reported disagreeing about finances a few times a month.

I don't share these statistics to scare you but to show you that almost every marriage struggles with finances, and we need to do our part, through prayer, to lessen our husbands' burden (as well as our own).

Praying God's Word When He Is Overwhelmed by Finances

Let us hold unswervingly to the hope we profess, for he who promised is faithful. (Heb. 10:23)

Father, I lift my husband to you, asking you to hold him firmly in your loving hands. I ask that you would protect his hope in you. Give him the strength to hold firmly to the hope he has in your love and the promises you have for him in your Word. I pray that in this time of exhaustion and overwhelming emotion, you would remind him through your Spirit of your faithfulness to him. I thank you in advance for restoring and renewing his spirit in you.

Like most men, my husband, Marty, is wired to be the provider for our family. Yet as he observed other "providers," his sense of worth screamed that he didn't measure up. I could tell he was thinking things like, "If I could just work harder, then I could have what Joe has. God expects me to provide!"

My prayer for Marty at that time was to see the truth of what Joe had. His marriage was a mess, he was in debt up to his knees, and he had walked away from following Christ, leaving his family broken. God took my prayers and revealed to Marty the truth. The Lord gently asked Marty, "Do you really want to be like Joe?"

Yes, God expects Marty to provide. But even more so, he expects Marty to turn to his provider and be as dependent on him as our family is on Marty.

God's words called to my husband, and he showed him great and wonderful things that caused Marty to take a chance and cry out. The result has been a love for these men he once envied, along with a desire to pour into them, and now I see him striving to be like Jesus instead of men.

Mimi

And my God will meet all your needs according to the riches of his glory in Christ Jesus. (Phil. 4:19)

Help my husband to remember that you will meet each and every need according to the riches of your glory, Jesus. All we have to do is ask and then rest in your loving, providing arms. Help me also to remember these words, and show me how I can help my husband in the work you have for us today. Thank you for your promises that you will meet our every need.

The LORD gives strength to his people;
the LORD blesses his people with peace. (Ps. 29:11)

I am asking today, dear Lord, for you to fill my husband with your peace concerning our finances. Give him the wisdom and strength to follow through on and solve the issues surrounding us right now. Show him the direction we need to go, and fill him with the peace of knowing that you will take good care of us, your children.

Overwhelmed by the Little Stuff

Men have a lot of strengths, but multitasking usually isn't one of them. When I'm working on my laptop, I tend to have about a dozen windows open at one time. I like flipping between the article I'm writing, my email, a website to find a recipe, a YouTube video of cats chasing their own shadows, and a Free Cell game.

If my husband or son needs to do something on my computer, the first thing they will do is ask me if they can close some of the windows. Just the fact that a window is open, asking for my guy's attention, makes him a little unsettled.

Most men have a harder time working with all the open "windows" in their lives than we do.

Praying God's Word When He Is Overwhelmed by the Little Stuff

Seek the LORD while he may be found;
call on him while he is near. (Isa. 55:6)

I fear the stress my husband is facing is pulling him further from you. Father, hear my prayer and draw him back to you. Help him seek you and call upon your name. Break the wall he has built. Chase him, Lord, and woo him back to you.

Come to me, all you who are weary and burdened, and I will give you rest. (Matt. 11:28)

My husband is weighted down by so many things. I pray that he would find rest in you, Lord. I pray for his sleep, that you would give him deep and restorative rest. I pray that when he does trust you with his burdens, they would not continue to weigh him down.

Being confident of this, that he who began a good work in you will carry it on to completion until the day of Christ Jesus. (Phil. 1:6)

Be with my husband today and give him the confidence he needs to withstand the emotions he's experiencing right now. Things are stacking up around him, and he feels like he is drowning in them. Dear Lord, remind him today that he is not alone, that you will see him through the work you're doing in him. We no longer need to strive to get things done because we have entered into your rest. Remind him of this so he can rest in your loving arms today.

Practical Steps

While praying God's Word is our most effective tool in supporting our husbands when they become overwhelmed, there are other practical steps we can take as well.

Remind him that he is not alone. One of the almost universal signs that a man is feeling inundated is that he will retreat—watching a lot of TV, not wanting to talk, hiding out in his "man cave," and generally avoiding contact with the human race. It's good to give your man some space during these times, but also remind him that when he needs you, you'll be there. Remind him that you are his partner in life and will support him in whatever way he needs.

Take some of the burden. If he's overwhelmed by finances, make sure you're taking every practical (and prayerful) step you can to increase income and reduce spending. Recently, when Roger was overwhelmed by our finances, I asked him what I could do to help. We had a serious discussion about what expenses were necessities and what needed to be dropped, even for a brief period of time. Since that time we have given up a lot of extras and reduced some of our necessities (at the grocery store I'm now squeezing a buck until it cries "Mama!"). While I know that staying within our budget takes some of the pressure off Roger, the fact that we're standing together, not fighting about the rules of the spending plan, gives him a lot of peace.

Build him up in other areas. When your man is feeling overwhelmed, his brain is probably spinning over all the areas in which he feels he's not measuring up. While there may not be a lot you can do to encourage him about work or other outside areas, you can encourage him in the areas you're involved in together. Here is what Robin says helps her husband:

> He has an increased need for physical intimacy and verbal reassurance during these times. I find that dropping phrases like "You take such good care of me," "You are such a good dad," and "I love the way you make me feel" seem to help get us through it.

Change your expectations. Recently I was speaking at an event and handing out these cute little bookmarks that say, "My husband is a hottie." I encouraged each woman not to use the bookmark in her books but to find a place where her husband could see the message on a regular basis—on the fridge, on his shaving mirror, in his car, etc. I handed the bookmark to one woman who looked at me and said, "I don't need a bookmark. My husband has been out of work for six months and has gained twenty-five pounds. He doesn't deserve a bookmark."

Ouch.

My husband usually gets overwhelmed when he is trying to do something—say, cook dinner—and the kiddos are underfoot no matter how hard I try to keep them out of the kitchen.

It may seem like a simple thing—getting a meal on the table with kids snapping at your ankles—but for some men, especially ones who have a harder time multitasking, it can be a source of frustration.

Vashie

I normally try to be very polite and understanding in these situations. Normally. Apparently I left my politeness at home that day. I looked her straight in the eye and said, "Now is the time your husband needs that silly little bookmark more than ever. I'm sure he's overwhelmed by not being able to find work and by gaining weight. He needs to know that you support him more than ever."

I don't know if what I said had any impact on her, but it was a good reminder for me. I can't wait to support my husband only when he is doing what I want him to do. My support is not a reward for him doing a good job—it is required as an act of love no matter the circumstances.

6

Employment

Four things let us ever keep in mind: God hears prayer, God heeds prayer, God answers prayer, and God delivers by prayer.

E. M. Bounds

One of my big insecurities has always been employment—specifically, about the men in my life having a job. My dad was either unemployed or underemployed ever since I was in third grade, and my first husband spent the last couple of years of our marriage without a job. So when I married Roger, I thought I'd hit the employment jackpot. He had worked for a major computer firm for over twenty years. Job security! Hurrah!

Yeah—not so much. Two days after we got home from our honeymoon, there was an all-hands-on-deck meeting where it was announced that a major portion of Roger's section was going to be laid off. Being an engineer in the Silicon Valley was a huge advantage in the nineties. Now the market is flooded with talented engineers, and the jobs are moving to other parts of the country or overseas. It was an excellent reminder for me not to trust in the things the world has to offer but to trust only in the Lord.

Having a paycheck at the end of the month is just one of the areas where we can cover our husband's career needs in prayer. Since our men are going to spend a major portion of their hours here on earth working, it's a good idea to spend a major portion of our prayer time on that subject.

Unemployed or Underemployed

I think one of the hardest things on a man—and a marriage—is unemployment. In my first marriage, my husband went through a two-year stint of not having a job, and the pain of and frustration with the lack of finances, direction, and purpose took a huge toll not only on our relationship but also on our family.

My friend Emily's husband, Gregg, is in the volatile real estate industry. Sometimes things are going great. Other times, when the economy is struggling and people are not buying like they used to, it's a huge strain. Here is what Emily has to say about how Gregg feels during these times:

> This is such a difficult area for men. So much of their self-worth is tied to being able to provide. I've seen so many men get depressed when they lose their job or their way to provide. My husband tends to fall back on David at times like these. David went through so much, and a lot of it is written down for us in the Bible. My prayer for Gregg when he feels lost or frustrated or inadequate is that he will find his worth in the promises of God—promises to give us hope and a future (Jer. 29:11). I LOVE David's prayer in 2 Samuel 7:18–29. My prayer for him based on that Scripture goes something like this:

Sovereign Lord, you are mighty. You are holy. You are the strength that my husband needs right now. I ask that your mighty hand will uphold him, guide him, and show him your ways. He feels small, he feels weak, and he feels alone. Help him to know he is not alone, but that you, the Creator of the world, are beside him, and that with you on his team, he can do anything. God, help him to feel your power and your promises. You never go back on your word, and you have promised to be with him. Send your Spirit, the Comforter, to be with him now in this troubled time.

Praying God's Word When He Is Unemployed or Underemployed

I trust in you;
>   do not let me be put to shame,
>   nor let my enemies triumph over me.
No one who hopes in you
>   will ever be put to shame,
but shame will come on those
>   who are treacherous without cause.
Show me your ways, LORD,
>   teach me your paths.
Guide me in your truth and teach me,
>   for you are God my Savior,
>   and my hope is in you all day long.
Remember, LORD, your great mercy and love,
>   for they are from of old. (Ps. 25:2–6)

My husband feels so much shame because of his work situation. I pray that my husband would put his hope in you and would never feel shame. I pray that he would seek you out and see only the truth of his life in you.

But now, Lord, what do I look for?
>   My hope is in you. (Ps. 39:7)

I pray that my husband and I will stop looking for hope and security in the world. I want our first response to be to look to you.

Why, my soul, are you downcast?
  Why so disturbed within me?
Put your hope in God,
  for I will yet praise him,
    my Savior and my God. (Ps. 42:11)

Don't let my husband get overtaken with depression, God. Turn him toward you. I pray as he looks for a job that we never put our hope in his income, but only, always in you.

Sustain me, my God, according to your promise, and I will live;
  do not let my hopes be dashed. (Ps. 119:116)

My husband is so easily discouraged right now, God. I pray that we will see evidence of your promises in every area of his life.

There is surely a future hope for you,
  and your hope will not be cut off. (Prov. 23:18)

My husband feels cut off, without a future. God, show him that he has a future. You see his future where we do not. Fill him with your hope.

7

Work Issues

One of the adversary's most useful schemes is to keep Christians focusing on their problems rather than on God's provision.

John R. Cionca

My husband works hard, but at the end of the day, he tries to be done. Not so for many of my friends' husbands. I have had several friends who have been frustrated and even angry about the amount of hours their husbands work.

Praying God's Word When He Works Too Much

Do everything without grumbling or arguing, so that you may become blameless and pure, "children of God without fault in a warped and crooked generation." Then you will shine among them like stars in the sky as you hold firmly to the word of life. And then I will be able to boast on the day of Christ that I did not run or labor in vain. But even if I am

My husband works a lot. And by a lot, I mean seventy-hour weeks with a five a.m. leave time, and coming home after the kids go to bed more often than not. And if I'm being honest, I'm not the best sport about it.

I know he's doing it for me and for our family. He grew up in a family where money was tight. He never had nice jeans or new shoes or dinners out in fancy restaurants. He worked his way through college, scraping together every penny to pay for tuition and books. And in the process, he made a vow to himself that he would always work hard to provide for his family. Before we got married, I remember him telling me that he would make sure I would always have the money I needed to pay the mortgage or buy a new pair of shoes. At the time, I appreciated that. Now I'm not so sure.

It's not that I don't like the assurance that there's money in the bank, but at the end of a long day, when I've been home all day with two whiny toddlers and an eighty-pound golden retriever, money isn't all that comforting. I need someone to help me wrangle my three-year-old into her pajamas. I need someone to feed the dog and fold that last load of

being poured out like a drink offering on the sacrifice and service coming from your faith, I am glad and rejoice with all of you. So you too should be glad and rejoice with me. (Phil. 2:14–18)

Lord, even when the days are long and I feel shorthanded, help me to go about the day without grumbling or arguing. Help me to be blameless and pure when it comes to my attitude about my husband. Help me to be uplifting and kind and generous with my praise even laundry and help me get dinner on the table. I need adult conversation. I need him. At home. Not at the office.

Of course, my grumpy attitude when he finally makes it home doesn't help. Instead of walking in the door to a just-nuked dinner and a quiet house, he often comes home to chaos. To the kids refusing to go to sleep. To toys all over the floor. And to me harping at him for being late (again).

I've been trying to think about this from his perspective. Here he works hard every day to provide for our family. He sets his alarm before five a.m. to go to his high-pressure, cut-throat job where no one is on his side. Then he comes home and finds himself isolated and living in chaos as I chastise him for being gone. That's so unfair—to him and to our family.

Over the last few years, I've spent a lot of time praying for him—that he'd see the light and start working less and coming home earlier. But I'm starting to realize that only by changing my attitude and looking at my own heart will I truly learn to love my husband. And so I'm going to start praying for him by praying for myself. Because the truth is, I'm the one who needs the change of heart.

Erin

when I'm feeling exhausted and alone. I want to be a light, a refuge for my husband, a place he can turn to when the entire world seems dark. I want him to know he can run into my arms and he will find safety and comfort. Lord, help me to be willing to sacrifice for him. If that means getting up early or staying up late or spending my days cleaning up messes, I'm willing. I want to rejoice in my marriage and in the man you gave me, just like I rejoice in you and the amazing gift you gave me at the cross.

Remember the Sabbath day by keeping it holy. Six days you shall labor and do all your work, but the seventh day is a sabbath to the Lord your God. On it you shall not do any work, neither you, nor your son or daughter, nor your male or female servant, nor your animals, nor any foreigner residing in your towns. (Exod. 20:8–10)

Thank you for showing my husband the importance of balancing work with the need for rest and relaxation. Lord, you have revealed this truth to him by your grace and mercy. When he is at rest, bring to his mind the very first Sabbath when you rested on the seventh day, and in his stillness and peace, may he draw ever closer to you.

Stress of the Job

Every job brings a certain amount of stress. But when your husband feels his heart racing or can't go to sleep at night, it's time to redouble your prayers in this area.

Praying God's Word When He Is under Stress at Work

Let the morning bring me word of your unfailing love,
    for I have put my trust in you.
Show me the way I should go,
    for to you I entrust my life. (Ps. 143:8)

Lord, I have noticed my husband is having some sleepless nights worrying over things at work. Remind my husband to do as King David did and pray. Remind him of your love for him in the morning. Remind him to let go of his thoughts for the night, and help him work through them with you in the morning. Also, remind him that he can put his total trust in you, and that when he does, you will guide him on the path you want him to go. Then he can believe you will help him make the right decisions.

Here's another way to pray this Scripture:

Let the morning bring my husband word of your unfailing love. Remind him to put his trust in you. Show him the way he should go, for he entrusts his life to you.

Wait for the LORD;
>   be strong and take heart
>   and wait for the LORD. (Ps. 27:14)

Lord, my husband has experienced being passed over repeatedly in promotions. He is feeling frustrated and angry. Help him to wait on you and your timing. Help him to be strong and take heart.

Or you might want to pray this version:

Lord, help my husband to wait for you. Help him to be strong and take heart and wait for you.

Keep this Book of the Law always on your lips; meditate on it day and night, so that you may be careful to do everything written in it. Then you will be prosperous and successful. (Josh. 1:8)

Lord, help my husband to keep your words always on his lips. Help him to meditate on the Bible day and night, so that he may be careful to do everything written in it. Then he will be prosperous and successful.

This is what the LORD says—
>   your Redeemer, the Holy One of Israel:
> "I am the Lord your God,
>   who teaches you what is best for you,
>   who directs you in the way you should go. (Isa. 48:17)

When the stress seems too much, O Lord, redeem my husband. Teach him what is best and direct him in the ways he should go.

Integrity at Work

Maybe it's a boss who asks your husband to cut corners, or another employee putting your husband in a situation to lie for her. Either way, your husband's integrity is one of the most important assets he has.

Praying God's Word for His Integrity at Work

Do your best to present yourself to God as one approved, a worker who does not need to be ashamed and who correctly handles the word of truth. (2 Tim. 2:15)

When criticisms or controversies arise at my husband's work, allow him to be the peacemaker between the factions. Give him the presence and composure to handle and resolve, with your blessing, any divisions that could result in distrust or misunderstanding. Let him speak your truth, gently but firmly, to those he discerns need guidance, and open his ears to the advice of others when given in love and understanding. Help him to rely on you and pray to you when the path is rough and the going is uncertain. Give him the grace to spread your Word through his actions and to stand tall in your unfailing love.

Don't cheat when measuring length, weight, or quantity. Use honest scales and weights and measures. I am GOD, your God. I brought you out of Egypt. (Lev. 19:35–36 Message)

Help my husband to always be honest in his job. Help him to stand firm with integrity by being honest to his boss, co-workers, and others he deals with every day.

Dishonest money dwindles away,
>but whoever gathers money little by little makes it grow.
>>(Prov. 13:11)

I pray, dear Lord, that you help my husband to be honest in all his dealings, to be a living example to others around him. Help him to be content to build our family's wealth over time. Help him to see your approval in the provision resulting from his hard work.

Success at Work

Emotionally healthy men have a couple of deep needs in their lives—to protect their families and to provide for them.

But with layoffs, downsizing, and a shifting workforce, your husband may not feel as secure in his career as he did a few years ago. Or maybe there are extra stresses at his job that he needs additional prayer for—a troublemaking co-worker, a pedantic boss, demanding deadlines, or unreasonable expectations.

Knowing that you have him covered in prayer can change the way your husband does his job—and gives him the confidence that comes from realizing that his wife loves him enough to take the time to pray for him.

Praying God's Word for His Success at Work

You will again obey the LORD and follow all his commands I am giving you today. Then the LORD your God will make you most prosperous in all the work of your hands and in the fruit of your womb, the young of your livestock and the crops of your land. The LORD will again delight in you and make you prosperous, just as he delighted in your ancestors, if you obey the LORD your God and keep his commands and decrees that are written in this Book of the Law and turn to the LORD your God with all your heart and with all your soul. (Deut. 30:8–10)

Lord, when my husband follows you and your commands, he is prosperous in all his work. You delight in him. I pray he turns to you today with all his heart and soul. Remind my husband that true success comes only from loving you with his whole being. Only then will he be successful.

Whatever you do, work at it with all your heart, as working for the Lord, not for human masters. (Col. 3:23)

Let my husband be ever mindful of your gracious hand in all his works. As he pours his heart into the projects and activities required by his job, remind him that it is you we work for, with gratitude for the many talents you have bestowed on us.

My husband is a youth pastor, and this greatly affects my prayers for him. There are so many areas that I feel the need to cover for him. I pray for his purity not only in his personal life but also in his ministry. I pray the passages in 1 Timothy 3 that pertain to overseers and deacons and list characteristics of good leaders.

I pray for him to be above reproach, faithful, temperate, self-controlled, respectable, hospitable, able to teach, not given to drunkenness, not violent, gentle, not argumentative, not greedy, a good manager of his household, and a great parent. My prayers often go like this:

Father, I lift my husband up to you. You have called him to this place of service. You have chosen him for this job at this place at this time, and I ask for your continued protection and blessing over him as he serves you in this way. I ask that you give him strength and boldness as he proclaims your Word. I pray that you give him patience as he deals with people.

God, I ask for you to guide him as he counsels others. May he always be faithful to you. I ask that you protect him from temptation and give him loads of self-control so that he can be accountable to others and to you. May he always be above reproach in his actions and his thoughts. Make him a gentle man, one who knows how to treat others with tenderness and respect. Help him to be the leader that you have called him to be. All praise be yours.

Amy

His Career Calling

I've known several men who held jobs they were not passionate about. What if your husband is fully and gainfully employed but not doing what he feels he was created to do?

Praying God's Word for His Career Calling

But be sure to fear the LORD and serve him faithfully with all your heart; consider what great things he has done for you. (1 Sam. 12:24)

Help my husband to be ever mindful of the great work you have begun in him. Let him always know that fear of you is the beginning of wisdom, and the gifts he has are not of his own making but ones you have bestowed on him. Allow him to serve you faithfully with all his heart, soul, and mind in every task he undertakes. Remind him, O Lord, of the great things you have done for him, and that his greatest accomplishment in life can be none other than serving you.

Those who work their land will have abundant food,
    but those who chase fantasies have no sense. (Prov. 12:11)

I pray that you give my husband a sound mind, not one full of dreams of success and wealth. Help him to withstand the pursuit of dreams or fantasies directing him this way and that and to stand firm on your correct path for his life. Help him to work hard, pursuing excellence in all he does to honor you, instead of pursuing a get-rich-quick scheme. Show him the right path and help him to stay on it.

From the fruit of their lips people are filled with good things,
    and the work of their hands brings them reward. (Prov. 12:14)

I pray, dear Lord, that you will enable my husband to communicate clearly. Fill his mouth with words that honor you and others, and give him the ability to work hard. Help him to see your reward for his faithfulness to you.

I feel the greatest need to pray for my husband's occupation. He's an ordained pastor, but that's not his current job. He'd love to get back into ministry full-time. He dislikes his current job so much that he feels defeated.

Paul has been affected spiritually and emotionally in this situation. He feels that he can be doing more for the Lord. He wants to be used for the kingdom, and I have to keep reminding him that God is using him, just in different ways right now. I think the hardest part is that we attend a church where we know lots of people on staff, and more and more of his friends are being hired—but he is not. I tell him that God hasn't guaranteed that he will be on staff at a local church, and he may direct us elsewhere.

I think all this has taken a toll on Paul's self-esteem, and he feels overwhelmed. I know it's affected our marriage because I don't see him leading in the way I know he can. It's hard to talk about this with my husband, who I know should be leading but doesn't.

Samantha

All hard work brings a profit,
    but mere talk leads only to poverty. (Prov. 14:23)

I want my husband to have dreams, dreams only you can accomplish, Lord, but when he is more talk than action, I know the outcome doesn't please you. Give my husband your discernment, God. And if he is afraid to take action because of his fear of failure, give him your boldness!

In everything that [Hezekiah] undertook in the service of God's temple and in obedience to the law and the commands, he sought his God and worked wholeheartedly. And so he prospered. (2 Chron. 31:21)

Remind my husband that like Hezekiah, when he works whole-heartedly and follows your commands, he will prosper in all that he does. In the ministry you have called him to—his career and his role as husband and father—help him to seek your will and work wholeheartedly in his service to you.

Do not work for food that spoils, but for food that endures to eternal life, which the Son of Man will give you. For on him God the Father has placed his seal of approval. (John 6:27)

Help my husband to measure his growth with you, Lord, as the way he measures success in his career. Help him to place as much importance on learning and growing with you as he does on his job.

8

When He Feels Inadequate

Do not pray for easy lives: Pray to be stronger men.
Do not pray for tasks equal to your powers. Pray for
powers equal to your task.

Phillips Brooks

Who doesn't love a capable man?

On a recent date night, Roger and I went to see a "boy movie." A boy movie is any movie where the main characters spend more time shooting each other than talking to each other, the leading man rides a motorcycle, and I have to hide my eyes more than twice as people throw knives at each other.

Roger and I have drastically different tastes in flicks, so when I expressed even a slight interest in a movie that involved international chases and exploding cars, Roger jumped on it. I can see why people enjoy these movies (and I possibly could as well—if the main character would stop getting shot). The main guys never hesitate about what to do—and they are never wrong. Bonus—they always have the right weapons with them! Their guns never run out of bullets, the group of bad guys waits their turn in order to fight them, and they are irresistible in a bad-boy sort of way.

In the cold light of day, that's not very realistic, is it? And yet I sometimes think these are the very standards that men are held to by society, wives, and the men themselves.

I have seen it over and over with women and romance novels, soap operas, and bad reality television. I'm all about a good love story, but I've seen a correlation between women who are not happy in their marriages and the consumption of those types of books and television shows. If we are feeding ourselves a constant diet of over-the-top romance, drama, and unobtainable expectations, we are going to communicate that to our husbands.

It's a vicious cycle. We feel something is missing in our own relationship, so we turn to that novel or TV romance for a quick hit—a little drama injected into our lives. The problem is those people are falling head over heels in love without any of the reality—they never have Visa bills to pay or kids that need to be taken to the orthodontist. So when our husbands don't send a dozen roses to our office or whisk us away from "all this" for a surprise trip to Aruba, there can rise in us a subtle dissatisfaction. A little "hmmm" that our husbands can't help but notice. And though they know they're doing something wrong, they don't know what it is.

But our homes should be the place where our husbands come to get filled up, not torn down—where our husbands know, in no uncertain terms, that they are enough. Let's be clear—no one at his work is telling him, "Great spreadsheet, Bill! You really rocked this assignment!" For most men, work is not a place to be affirmed and encouraged. It is a place to do their jobs, to hopefully not get noticed when things go wrong, and to bring home a paycheck.

Men feeling inadequate is nothing new. Even Moses, the leader of a great nation, didn't feel up to his task. In a burning bush, God appeared to him and said, "So now, go. I am sending you to Pharaoh to bring my people the Israelites out of Egypt" (Exod. 3:10). Moses was understandably shaken with the vision and the responsibility. He stalled because he knew he was not up to the task. He explained to God that he was not able to speak well and knew he couldn't do what God was asking of him.

> Moses said to the LORD, "Pardon your servant, Lord. I have never been eloquent, neither in the past nor since you have spoken to your servant. I am slow of speech and tongue."
> The LORD said to him, "Who gave human beings their mouths? Who makes them deaf or mute? Who gives them sight or makes them blind? Is it not I, the LORD? Now go; I will help you speak and will teach you what to say." (Exod. 4:10–12)

So God provided Moses with two things: a rod that would help him perform miracles and Aaron to speak for him. I see this story as an example of how God still provides for us today.

God asks us to do some big, hairy things. But he also provides everything we need for what he calls us to do. Our husbands may not have to lead a nation out of Egypt, but other areas of responsibility can be daunting for them:

supporting a family in a bad economy

raising kids in a world that isn't interested in what is best for them being a godly man in a world filled with corruption

standing up to shady business practices

loving his wife faithfully

In the face of all these demands, there are probably not a whole lot of people around our husbands supporting them. However, there are plenty of people in the world who take great delight in tearing them down. Whether it is advertisements directed at them to make them feel "less than," or the unintended legacy of a harsh parent, there are many things that can make our men feel inadequate.

But God did not intend for us to live up to the world's impossible standards or even those of an unpleasable parent. God's desire is for each of us to know our worth in him.

Praying God's Word When He Feels Inadequate

Peace I leave with you; my peace I give you. I do not give to you as the world gives. Do not let your hearts be troubled and do not be afraid. (John 14:27)

Please leave your peace in my husband's spirit. Help him to see himself not the way the world sees him but how you see him. Remove his troubled spirit and his feelings of inadequacy. Fill him with your wisdom and knowledge, and help him to rely on the peace you've promised. Help me to be the wife he needs, encouraging him and lifting him up in the way you have called me to.

The LORD is my strength and my defense;
    he has become my salvation.
He is my God, and I will praise him,
    my father's God, and I will exalt him. (Exod. 15:2)

I pray that you provide strength for my husband and also a joy that can be found only in a relationship with you. I pray that my husband's every word and deed is focused on bringing you pleasure and praise because you are worthy.

It is God who arms me with strength
and keeps my way secure. (2 Sam. 22:33)

*My husband so often wants to rely on his own strength. Father,
I pray he would see that you have the perfect plan for his life, and
you will give him the strength to carry it out.*

For the eyes of the LORD range throughout the earth to
strengthen those whose hearts are fully committed to him.
(2 Chron. 16:9)

*Let my husband know that you are always "seeing around cor-
ners" for him, that he is never alone, and that you are strengthening
him every day.*

Though I walk in the midst of trouble,
you preserve my life.
You stretch out your hand against the anger of my foes;
with your right hand you save me.
The Lord will vindicate me;
your love LORD, endures forever—
do not abandon the works of your hands. (Ps. 138:7–8)

*Lord, you know the areas my husband is struggling with right
now. He is walking in the midst of trouble. Please revive him. Thank
you for stretching forth your hand against the wrath of his enemy.
It is not his job, his place, or his lack of placement in church that
is the issue. It is the enemy seeking to destroy his confidence. Lord,
you know what concerns him. Would you accomplish your will in
this area? I know you will because you love my husband even more
than I do, and that love is everlasting. Help him to see that he is the
work of your hands and you will not forsake that work.*

But you, LORD, do not be far from me.
You are my strength; come quickly to help me. (Ps. 22:19)

*I know that sometimes my husband struggles to feel your presence.
Lord, demonstrate your strength to him! When he feels overwhelmed
and underequipped, come quickly to him.*

Inadequacy . . . I believe this affects a husband strongly, as he is the head of the household. The responsibility to provide security for his wife and children is so high. And as a Christian man, the responsibility to lead spiritually adds yet another layer to his life.

When Gregg feels inadequate, he turns inward. He is not as vivacious, lacks desire to initiate family activities, and becomes less engaged in home life. Many times he doubts his actions. This is especially true in parenting. He wonders if he said the right words of encouragement or correction. He wonders if he is living by example as a godly man. When our boys are making good decisions, Gregg feels more confident. But when they choose paths that are not desirable, that eats him up like a caterpillar eats a spring leaf! He is perplexed at what he taught them, what he said, what he didn't say. He feels inadequate.

When Gregg is feeling this way, I try to extend grace and comfort. I remind him that it is God who is ultimately in control of our finances, his business, and the children. I try to be a good listener, because Gregg processes by talking things out. Sometimes I want to say, "No, no! You are a great father/husband/boss!" But if he doesn't feel that way, it rings hollow. So I patiently listen. I affirm how he is feeling. I reveal my inadequacies too.

But what I think helps most is paying attention to his needs. Sometimes when he separates himself from the family, I get offended. But instead of being miffed and thus ignoring him, I try to see if maybe he's troubled by something and come alongside. I may rub his back or say, "Do you want to talk? Let's go for a walk." Or we'll go to a movie so he can escape in an adventure flick. The best remedy, though, is probably sex. If he knows I still desire to be with him, that I crave him, he feels less inadequate. Also, before the night ends, I ask, "Do you want to pray together?" As we close the night in unified prayer, asking God to be our guide, sleep comes more readily. One of our favorite passages during these times of inadequacy is Psalm 63:1–8. I pray it this way:

> O God, my God, I earnestly search for you on behalf of my husband. His soul thirsts for you, and his whole body longs for you and your guidance. This parched land that he's walking through makes him feel dried up, weak, and so inadequate. He has seen you in your sanctuary and knows full well your power and glory. May that power sustain him even now. May your unfailing love give him hope and life. Your love is so good, I can't stop shouting about it! Be his satisfaction, more than the best meal at his favorite restaurant. Turn his mind toward you at night when he worries about the problems of the day. Be his helper. With your strong right hand, hold him securely. May he cling to you, O God, my God!

Emily

My soul is weary with sorrow;
  strengthen me according to your word. (Ps. 119:28)

Your Word says that you are my husband's strength, even now as he feels weak, Lord. He desperately needs you to carry him. God, I pray that you would strengthen his soul.

So do not fear, for I am with you;
  do not be dismayed, for I am your God.
I will strengthen you and help you;
  I will uphold you with my righteous right hand. (Isa. 41:10)

God, my husband needs to be held up today. He is fearful and frustrated and does not feel equal to his task. I know you are sufficient to meet all of his needs, so let him feel your presence in a tangible way today.

The LORD will guide you always;
  he will satisfy your needs in a sun-scorched land
  and will strengthen your frame.
You will be like a well-watered garden,
  like a spring whose waters never fail. (Isa. 58:11)

My husband feels dry and used up, yet in you he can be restored. He seems to be a shell of who he has been in the past. Strengthen his body and soul, provide for his needs, and let him be overflowing in joy every day of his life.

But now, this is what the LORD says—
  he who created you, Jacob,
  he who formed you, Israel:
"Do not fear, for I have redeemed you;
  I have summoned you by name; you are mine.
When you pass through the waters,
  I will be with you;
and when you pass through the rivers,

they will not sweep over you.
When you walk through the fire,
   you will not be burned;
   the flames will not set you ablaze.
For I am the Lord your God,
   the Holy One of Israel, your Savior." (Isa. 43:1–3)

When my husband feels swept over by feelings of inadequacy, when he feels "burned" by the difference between who he wants to become and who he is right now, remind him that you created him, you formed him, you have redeemed and summoned him. His talents, abilities, and efforts are not his god or his savior; only you are. Help him to live secure in the knowledge that no matter who he is (or isn't), you always call him by name, and you call him yours.

The Sovereign LORD is my strength;
   he makes my feet like the feet of a deer,
   he enables me to tread on the heights. (Hab. 3:19)

Not by his strength but by yours, Lord, will my husband be able to tackle the high places and obstacles before him. I pray that he will know that you will not take him anywhere you are not present.

I can do all this through him who gives me strength. (Phil. 4:13)

Show my husband that anything you have appointed him to do, he can do in your strength.

Strengthen the feeble hands,
   steady the knees that give way. (Isa. 35:3)

My husband feels like he is getting too old for the type of work he does. Lord, please sustain him. Let him remember that wisdom trumps youth and that he is valued and valuable.

But he said to me, "My grace is sufficient for you, for my power is made perfect in weakness." Therefore I will boast all the more gladly about my weaknesses, so that Christ's power may rest on me. That is why, for Christ's sake, I delight in weaknesses, in insults, in hardships, in persecutions, in difficulties. For when I am weak, then I am strong. (2 Cor. 12:9–10)

Father, my husband is feeling weak and just not enough. Show him your strength. Let him understand that you don't look down on him because of his weaknesses but can use him because of them. Lord, let your strength fill him up.

9

His Finances

Pray like it all depends on God, but work like it all
depends on you. .

Dave Ramsey

There is a reason that Jesus spends more time talking about
money than any other subject in the New Testament. Throughout the ages—and most likely at your kitchen table—money
has caused more strife and wars than any other subject.

It causes a battle for the man in your life as well. Money
messes with the mind.

The Battleground of Money

When you think about all the things that we as married couples
can fight about—kids, work, in-laws, sex—the fact that we
fight most about money shows what a powerful force money
is in our lives. I know it's a big issue in my own marriage. My

mother was a planner when it came to finances. She wouldn't rest until she could account for that one-penny difference in the checkbook. My father struggled with holding a job after I entered high school, so the financial burden was put on my mom. She was a hero to me—holding down a full-time job, running our house, getting dinner on the table. All the while, she did without so that my brother and I could have some of the experiences that were important to us as kids.

But what that growing-up experience left me with was an anxiety about money. And what I have done—mostly unconsciously—is transfer that burden to Roger. If the money is fine, I don't say anything. If we're low on money before the end of the month, then I raise the tension. My poor husband ends up in a no-win situation.

And so many of us, including our husbands, have made big money mistakes that are hard to recover from:

> About fifteen years ago, Matt was bought out of a company. To get him "out," they gave him $250,000. The money should have set us for life, but instead he made two poor choices. One was to invest in a risky stock market. He put almost the entire amount in it. Within three months, it tanked and we lost it all. He was so desperate at this time that an elder in our church suggested he make a stand against the government and stop paying taxes. I hated this idea and fought him tooth and nail, but finally I let him take us down this dangerous road. This was worse than losing the $250,000. We had agents at our doors and penalties that followed us for years.
>
> We are free of this today, and Matt has realized his mistakes. I had to verbally forgive him over and over until he believed me, sought the Lord's forgiveness, and forgave himself.
>
> I know this story makes Matt sound terrible. He is a piece of work for sure—but one that Jesus has molded beautifully

into the man he is today. I wanted you to know that this is now past tense, but I still remember it vividly.

Missy

Here was Missy's Scripture and prayer during that time of great hurt and uncertainty, based on Psalm 51:10–12: *Lord, my husband has blown it! Yep, it's a big one. I'm mad, but I know your patience with me endures forever. Help me to have patience and lovingly pray for him to fall at your feet. Restore unto him the joy of your salvation, and renew a right spirit within him.*

Or maybe you just feel like no matter how hard you try, how careful you are, you and your husband can never get ahead:

> Recently while doing our taxes, we were told that we have been doing them wrong for eight years. Because my husband is a minister, there is a lot of confusion regarding his tax status. When he came home and shared with me that we owed more than $10,000 to the IRS, I felt like I'd been sucker punched. After the initial blow, I was ready to have a Pollyanna attitude and roll up my sleeves to figure our way out of the debt. I could tell, however, that he was still very weighed down. This was supposed to be our "year of no" so that we could be out of debt by November, except for the house. It had felt so good to be almost done! Then to add half again what we owe to our cumulative debts was staggering.
>
> My husband is by no means depressed, but I can tell how difficult this is for him. My prayer during this time springs out of the story of the widow of Zarephath, who provided for Elijah in 1 Kings 17:7–16:
>
> *Father God, this is a very difficult time. You know our situation in its fullness. You also know the strain and stress finances can cause in life. I lift up my husband to you right now and ask that you give him the strength he needs to endure and to think clearly regarding our situation. Help me*

to do what I can to ease his burden, to be even wiser with how I spend our money. Help me to employ all my frugal know-how to make our resources stretch further.

God, I pray that you provide the same way you provided for the widow of Zarephath. Help my husband to remain steadfast. Thank you that he is a man of integrity. Help us to trust you and lean fully on you during this time of financial difficulty. We do not serve two gods; we serve only you, so do not let these issues with money discourage us. We will give to Caesar what is Caesar's and to you what is yours!

We love you so much, Father, and we thank you for your continued blessings.

Tracy

Praying God's Word on Finances

Do not be one who shakes hands in pledge
    or puts up security for debts;
if you lack the means to pay,
    your very bed will be snatched from under you.
     (Prov. 22:26–27)

Father, it is so tempting to live beyond our means when we see everyone around us with more than we have. Teach us to live within our means. Help us not to be tempted by going after more than you want for us. Let our satisfaction in life come from you.

You will be enriched in every way so that you can be generous on every occasion, and through us your generosity will result in thanksgiving to God. (2 Cor. 9:11)

Compared to the majority of this world, we are so very rich. Dear Lord, remind both my husband and myself daily of how rich we are so on every occasion you bring to us, we can be generous in response. You tell us that you will give us an overabundance so we can be generous to others around us, and when we do, it results in praise to you. Therefore help us not to forget that, so we will not stumble by being selfish toward others around us.

But seek first his kingdom and his righteousness, and all these things will be given to you as well. Therefore do not worry about tomorrow, for tomorrow will worry about itself. Each day has enough trouble of its own. (Matt. 6:33–34)

Dear Lord, you tell us that when we seek you first, everything will be provided for us. Help my husband to remember this and not fret about the bills and how they are going to be paid. Help him to set them aside, concentrate on a relationship with you, and seek your will, knowing that all things work out for those who love you. Help him not to worry about the future but to rest in your peace and understanding and to fully trust you to guide us in our financial situation.

Here's another prayer based on this Scripture:

Remind my husband to seek first your kingdom and your righteousness, and all these things will be given to him as well. Remind him not to worry about tomorrow, for tomorrow will worry about itself. Each day has enough trouble of its own.

Dishonest money dwindles away,
    but whoever gathers money little by little makes it grow.
      (Prov. 13:11)

I pray that you help my husband stay faithful to you. Help him to be honest in all his dealings and to be a living example to others around him. By moving forward on the path you have set before him, may he see your approval in the prosperous provision resulting from his hard work.

When You Don't Agree on Finances

Maybe you are the spender, and your husband recycles the aluminum foil. Or maybe his trips to the Bass Pro Shop are quickly leading toward you living in his boat. Whenever a couple doesn't agree on how to spend (and save) money, it can lead to a lot of stress, frustration, and discontentment.

My husband is nuts about Disney. He grew up in Florida, and his strongest memories are tied to that magic kingdom. Before we got married, Roger and his kids had annual passes to Disneyland—about a seven-hour car trip from our house—and made the pilgrimage a minimum of four times a year.

Once we got married, Roger was all set to keep up his pace of quarterly trips to see Mickey. But with the debt from my previous marriage, things were going to be pretty lean. Both of us had issues with spending (mine leaned more toward shoes than travel), and neither of us really enjoyed handling finances. But after a couple of years of pretty unaccountable spending, we had to have some serious discussions about all things financial.

During one of those conversations, I asked Roger what it was about the Disney experience that he loved so much. He said, "I just love the feeling of being there—for a little while feeling like I have money. Staying at the Grand Californian and being taken care of and treated well. I just love everything about it." That makes a lot of sense coming from a dad who was single for thirteen years. There weren't a lot of people in his life saying, "How are you doing? Is there something I can do for you?" On the other hand, I still don't think Roger sees my need for world shoe domination as reasonable. We've had to talk through finances and come to a "one mind" kind of place concerning them. Prayer works. So does Dave Ramsey's *The Total Money Makeover*. (Just saying.)

Praying God's Word When You Don't Agree on Finances

Trust in the LORD with all your heart
    and lean not on your own understanding.
in all your ways submit to him,
    and he will make your paths straight. (Prov. 3:5–6)

Lord, help my sweet husband to know what it means to trust—to live fully and wholly in the confidence of your faithfulness. Father, help my husband to see you as the perfect abba he never had. Help him to know that with all of his heart, he can put his hope in your faithfulness.

Father, we know that our perspective is so limited—we cannot possibly see or understand what you can. Help my husband to put his trust in you even when our future is vague and uncertain, and to know with confidence that you will deliver on your promise to light our way and make straight our path.

Every good and perfect gift is from above, coming down from the Father of the heavenly lights, who does not change like shifting shadows. (James 1:17)

Lord, sometimes my husband forgets that every good and perfect gift is from you. The world is pulling at him and tells him the many ways he does not measure up. Hold him extra close at these times so he can hear your heartbeat. Allow each beat to reveal more of you as he strives to die to self.

10

His Health and Safety

Worry does not empty tomorrow of its sorrow. It empties today of its strength.

Corrie ten Boom

My husband and his son, Jeremy, like to do outdoorsy things like camping and watching meteor showers. Me? My stargazing consists of watching three Sandra Bullock movies in a row.

So I am more than happy to let the men be men and go on their overnight adventures. My only problem? Cell phone reception.

On these road trips Roger is often out of cell range, and just knowing that I can't get ahold of him makes me a little antsy. Or, if I'm being completely honest, a bit worried. If I don't combat my worrying over my husband's health and safety right away, my mind starts to fill in the blanks and I become like a dog with a bone. I gnaw on the worry and turn it over and walk away and come right back to it. I get distracted from other things in my life because I'm worried.

I know that worry is the antithesis of trusting God. It is the polar opposite of what I should be doing. When I replace prayer with worry, I am fighting God for control of my husband.

Whether he is a military man who is in harm's way on a daily basis or an engineer driving home after a long day at work, a husband's physical safety is a priority for every wife I know. At some point in each of our lives, there is going to be a bad doctor's report, a phone call from the emergency room, or a cell phone call that starts out, "Honey, I want you to know it's going to be okay, but . . ." It is important that we are praying for our husbands before we get the call—praying for God's protection over them each and every day. There is no safer place for our husbands to be than in God's hands.

Covering Him in Every Area

Praying for my husband physically doesn't just concern fender benders and dire illnesses; I also pray for Roger when he is feeling run-down or exhausted, when he has a headache or just a cold. Part of my job as his wife is to take care of him when he is under the weather, and that includes praying for him. We are at the point in our marriage where I know what gets my husband down physically—long hours at work, the events he runs at church, stressful projects, and lack of sleep. Knowing my husband's rhythms of work and sleep, as well as his schedule, gives me a lot of information on how to pray for him.

Worry about His Safety

Roger had to help me carry some of my emotional baggage when we were first married.

In my previous marriage, my husband had been working overseas in England when I got the call. "He's been in a head-on collision, and the prognosis isn't good." After several more phone calls and grave discussions with doctors, I boarded a plane to London the next day. I didn't know if I was going to pick up my husband or bring back his body.

After several days in a coma, several weeks in the hospital, and several months off work, he made a full recovery. But that didn't lessen the effect that incident had on my level of fear—something I had a hard time letting go of in my marriage to Roger.

This was a real sticking point with Roger and me after we were married. He would be five minutes late getting home, and I would be frantically calling his cell and imagining ambulances and tangled steel.

Part of the reason that I need to be praying specifically for Roger's safety is to make sure not only that he is covered in prayer, but also that I am not taking on God's job as his protector.

In those first years, Roger saw my constant need to know where he was every moment of the day not as loving but as controlling. And now that I look back on it, if I had really given God the authority in my life, I would have realized that I had no control over the situation. I needed to keep Roger firmly in God's hands instead of trying to control him in his day-to-day comings and goings.

My prayers are effective. My worry is not. Praying Scripture is my biggest weapon against worry. It is a reminder of God's promises of provision and protection. Let me suggest that if you struggle with worry like I do, spend some time meditating on the Scriptures in this section and choose one to memorize. When that struggle starts to well up in you, and you have those feelings of unrest and anxiety, use God's words to combat what Satan is trying to do—create a lack of peace in you.

Praying God's Word for His Safety

Do not be anxious about anything, but in every situation, by prayer and petition, with thanksgiving, present your requests to God. (Phil. 4:6)

Lord, I choose the path of peace instead of anxiety by thanking you, praying to you, and asking you for what I need.

Cast all your anxiety on him because he cares for you. (1 Pet. 5:7)

I give you every fear and anxiety I am struggling with right now. I know that you love and care for me and my husband, and you will carry these burdens for me.

They will have no fear of bad news;
    their hearts are steadfast, trusting in the LORD. (Ps. 112:7)

I so often borrow bad news with worry over things I can't control. Help me to trust you daily for every outcome.

Praying God's Word for Protection over Your Husband

While traveling and speaking with my first book, *The Husband Project*, I have had several opportunities to connect with wives whose husbands have been deployed overseas. I know that these women carry a special burden of prayer for their husbands who are facing real danger—sometimes on a daily basis. I asked some of my friends from PWOC (Protestant Women of the Chapel) which verses of protection were most meaningful to them as they prayed for our military men. Several women said that Psalm 121 gives them great comfort both when their husbands are deployed and when they are serving stateside. I can see why that Psalm is used by so many military wives as a prayer for their husbands. The assurance that at all times their husbands are under God's watch is powerful to women who have no control over the circumstances their husbands are in.

I also love the image and the promise of God's protection in Psalm 91, and the prayers that it inspires:

> Whoever dwells in the shelter of the Most High
>   will rest in the shadow of the Almighty.
> I will say of the LORD, "He is my refuge and my fortress,
>   my God, in whom I trust." (Ps. 91:1–2)

I pray that my husband would dwell in you, the shelter of the Most High, and will abide in your almighty shadow. I pray that he would recognize you as his refuge and his fortress and that he would trust in you.

This protection is not up to us. As I use that verse to pray for my husband, I pray that he would seek God's protection and trust in the Lord.

Here are some additional verses from Psalm 91 that you could use to pray for your husband's protection:

> If you say, "The LORD is my refuge,"
>   and you make the Most High your dwelling,
> no harm will overtake you,
>   no disaster will come near your tent.
> For he will command his angels concerning you
>   to guard you in all your ways. (Ps. 91:9–11)

I pray that my husband would look to you for his protection, that he would not be harmed or overtaken. May he be able to sleep in peace at night because of your protection. I pray that your angels, who are under your command, will guard him at every turn.

"Because he loves me," says the Lord, "I will rescue him;
    I will protect him, for he acknowledges my name.
He will call on me, and I will answer him;
    I will be with him in trouble,
    I will deliver him and honor him.
With long life I will satisfy him
    and show him my salvation." (Ps. 91:14–16)

Father, I pray that my husband would know in the deepest part of his being your love for him, and that he would love you as well. I pray that he would call on your name, and even when he can't hear you, that he would feel your presence—especially when he is in dangerous situations. I pray for your protection on him, both physically and spiritually.

Praying More of God's Word for His Protection

For the Lord will be at your side
    and will keep your foot from being snared. (Prov. 3:26)

I pray that you protect each of my husband's steps today—physically, mentally, and spiritually. I pray he would not be one step outside of your will and would not stumble into anything that is not from you.

I lie down and sleep;
    I wake again, because the Lord sustains me. (Ps. 3:5)

I pray that my husband will be free from worry and be able to sleep deeply and well, knowing it's you who sustains him.

Many women shared with me that not only do they pray these verses over their husbands, but they also create physical reminders of God's protection. One woman created a quilt with camouflage squares and stitched verses onto the fabric. Another woman told me about Operation Bandana (www.operationbandana.org), which sends out camouflage bandanas with Psalm 91 imprinted on them.

Acts 17:26 may not seem really obvious as a "comfort verse." But it has brought me a great deal of comfort not only for deployments but for military life in general. It helps me understand that no matter where I am or where my husband is, God has set the time and place of our lives. So no matter where we go, whether together or apart, God has planned it and has it all under his control.

Cheryl, military wife

Most of us don't have husbands serving in the military, but we can take our cues from women who do. When it comes to praying for safety and protection, these women recognize the real danger their husbands are in but are able to release them into God's hands.

Praying When Your Husband Is Sick or Injured

I have to tell you, this physical area is one where I struggle—it is the hardest for me to pray boldly and expectantly. I believe in God's healing power and his ability to protect, but I have to fight with doubt when I am praying for people I love.

I have seen so many people who have prayed for themselves and for others who have not been healed as I had hoped or expected. These instances have left me confused, disappointed, and sometimes even angry with God.

But then there have been those other times—times when I have prayed for a friend or a family member and have seen miraculous, inexplicable healing and restoration.

I don't understand why some are physically healed and some are not. I have searched the Scriptures and read books on the subject, and I still don't know the reasoning. I don't think that anyone can say why with certainty. That is why I so identify with the father in Mark 9:14–24:

> When they came to the other disciples, they saw a large crowd around them and the teachers of the law arguing with them. As soon as all the people saw Jesus, they were overwhelmed with wonder and ran to greet him.
> "What are you arguing with them about?" he asked.
> A man in the crowd answered, "Teacher, I brought you my son, who is possessed by a spirit that has robbed him of speech. Whenever it seizes him, it throws him to the ground. He foams at the mouth, gnashes his teeth and becomes rigid. I asked your disciples to drive out the spirit, but they could not."
> "You unbelieving generation," Jesus replied, "how long shall I stay with you? How long shall I put up with you? Bring the boy to me."
> So they brought him. When the spirit saw Jesus, it immediately threw the boy into a convulsion. He fell to the ground and rolled around, foaming at the mouth.
> Jesus asked the boy's father, "How long has he been like this?"
> "From childhood," he answered. "It has often thrown him into fire or water to kill him. But if you can do anything, take pity on us and help us."
> " 'If you can'?" said Jesus. "Everything is possible for one who believes."
> Immediately the boy's father exclaimed, "I do believe; help me overcome my unbelief!"

I love the contradiction in this father's cry to Jesus: "I believe, but help me because I don't believe!" Almost every time I pray for healing for someone, I have to start by personalizing verse 24 for myself: "God, I believe in your power to heal. Help me believe in this moment, for this person, right now." Fortunately, God understands our struggles and loves us despite them. We don't have to put on a show of believing for him. He understands the wrestling of our hearts and embraces us in the struggle. But one thing is clear: we need to pray. Whether it's a family history of heart disease or a bad head cold, nothing is too big or too small to bring to God.

Praying God's Word for Healing

LORD my God, I called to you for help,
    and you healed me. (Ps. 30:2)

God, there is nothing out of your reach and no part of my husband's body you cannot touch. We call on you for help and ask you to heal him.

Have mercy on me, LORD, for I am faint;
    heal me, LORD, for my bones are in agony. (Ps. 6:2)

God, my husband is so tired. Breathe life into him. Heal him from pain as only you can do.

11

His Relationship
with God

If I could hear Christ praying for me in the next room,
I would not fear a million enemies. Yet distance
makes no difference. He is praying for me.

Robert Murray McCheyne

I know my husband's strengths and weaknesses. I know his schedule and everything going on in his life. I know his past—his habits, his mistakes, his childhood. So when I think about Roger having a different kind of relationship with God, one that is deeper, fuller, and richer, I am almost afraid to pray, thinking I already know the outcome.

But only God can see around the corners of my husband's life. While I know my husband, God *knows* my husband. He knows what Roger needs in order to go deeper with him. He knows what breaks Roger's heart, and how far Roger will stray if left to his own devices. God knows my husband.

Another thing that makes me pull back from praying for my husband and his relationship with God is assuming he doesn't really need the prayer.

Roger has never been a rebellious guy. When we were talking about our childhoods recently, I asked him the worst thing he did as a kid. He told me that while spending the night at a friend's house, his friend talked him into taking a sip of ginger ale. Yes, naive little Roger thought that because they didn't have ginger ale at *his* house, there must have been something illicit about it.

Recently our church has been studying the story of the prodigal son in Luke 15:11–31. For so much of my life, I have identified with the younger son—not always living the way I should, being reckless, and running away from my father. But our pastor pointed out, "One was lost in rebellion, one was lost in religion." Both the younger and the older brother were lost. Now that was something Roger could identify with.

Roger has spent his whole life serving in the church, leading in the church, being part of the community. But for a man who has spent so much of his life serving God, Roger often has not felt close to him. Just like the older brother, Roger had never run away, but he also didn't feel like he had a relationship with God.

I think of it this way. I've had to replace my driver's license twice in my life: once when I left it behind in Japan, and two years later when I lost it back in the States. After replacing the second license, eventually I found the lost card. It had fallen in the slot of the cover of my emergency brake in my car. I had been driving around with that license not six inches away from me for over a year. But the funny thing? It was as lost as the license in Japan.

Just because Roger was still going to church and doing all the things he was "supposed" to do didn't mean that, at times, he wasn't just as lost as my friend's husband who shows up for church only when his daughter is singing in the children's choir.

Maybe your husband is lost in rebellion. Or maybe he has been lost in religion. Either way, it could be your prayer that moves him to be found again.

Praying God's Word for His Relationship with God

Trust in the LORD with all your heart
and lean not on your own understanding;
in all your ways submit to him,
and he will make your paths straight. (Prov. 3:5–6)

God, I know that my husband has tried to do things on his own. I pray that his first instinct would be to lean on you. You see around all the corners of his life. I pray that he would trust fully in you, asking you to lead every aspect of his life.

What, then, shall we say in response to these things? If God is for us, who can be against us? (Rom. 8:31)

My husband sometimes feels so alone. I pray that he would know that you are for him. He can stand against anything as long as he stands with you.

Understanding God's Love for Him

If any of us, including our husbands, began to understand even a portion of God's love for us, wouldn't it change everything in our lives? I love the prayer that my friend Adelle prays for her husband, Gabe. He's told her on several occasions how much it means to him that she prays these verses for him:

> You have searched me, LORD,
>> and you know me.
> You know when I sit and when I rise;
>> you perceive my thoughts from afar.
> You discern my going out and my lying down;
>> you are familiar with all my ways. (Ps. 139:1–3)

Abba Father, you know this man so intimately. You know his thoughts, his mind, his heart. Just as we watch our children and know every movement, every action, you watch him with the eyes of a careful, loving parent. Though I may know my husband so intimately that I can judge his mood by the very pace of his breath, oh, so much more do you know him and love him, Father.

> Where can I go from your Spirit?
>> Where can I flee from your presence?
> If I go up to the heavens, you are there;
>> if I make my bed in the depths, you are there.
> If I rise on the wings of the dawn,
>> if I settle on the far side of the sea,
> even there your hand will guide me,
>> your right hand will hold me fast.
> If I say, "Surely the darkness will hide me
>> and the light become night around me,"
> even the darkness will not be dark to you;
>> the night will shine like the day,
>> for darkness is as light to you. (Ps. 139:7–12)

Lord, though at times he may turn his face away from you and flee from your presence, I know you are with him. You run to him, and he cannot flee from a Father who loves him and knows him so well. When he is exploding with greatest joy, you are there. When he suffers with the deepest hurt, you are there. The moment he opens his eyes in the morning, you are by his side. Though at times he may feel invisible and lost in the gloom and darkness of uncertainty and fear, you are still there. What he sees as darkness is not darkness to you.

> I praise you because I am fearfully and wonderfully made;
>> your works are wonderful,
>> I know that full well.
> My frame was not hidden from you
>> when I was made in the secret place,
>> when I was woven together in the depths of the earth.
> Your eyes saw my unformed body;
>> all the days ordained for me were written in your book
>> before one of them came to be. (Ps. 139:14–16)

My husband is so beautiful to me, Lord. You created the perfect helpmate and companion for me. You fashioned his very form, lovingly shaping and molding him from the inside out. He was no accident, Lord; this I know so well. He was created with precision and intent, and you have plans for this man—big plans. Long before he took his first breath, you wrote his name on your hand. Every day of his life has been revealed to you—there is nothing hidden from your eyes. It comforts me, Lord, to know that my husband is and always will be in your sincerest care.

> Search me, God, and know my heart;
>> test me and know my anxious thoughts.
> See if there is any offensive way in me,
>> and lead me in the way everlasting. (Ps. 139:23–24)

Search and guard his heart, O Lord! Keep him from dangers of the mind, from temptations and lies that will shroud him in darkness. Cast away anxious thoughts that filter the truth, and lead him into the light. Pull away the cobwebs of fear and shine a bright light on his path. Reveal to him your perfect truth. Bring the darkest lies of the enemy into the brightest light where they cannot survive. Guard and guide him always, holy Father, and never, ever let him go.

Praying God's Word for Keeping Him Close to God

The Spirit himself testifies with our spirit that we are God's children. Now if we are children, then we are heirs—heirs of God and co-heirs with Christ, if indeed we share in his sufferings in order that we may also share in his glory. (Rom. 8:16–17)

My husband is your child, and your love for him is boundless. Comfort him in the knowledge that Christ suffered for him, and because of this, he is not alone in his suffering. Invite him to take your hand and walk by your side through the storm. Reveal to him, in the good times and bad, the glory that is yours alone.

Submit yourselves, then, to God. Resist the devil, and he will flee from you. Come near to God and he will come near to you. (James 4:7–8)

Help my husband keep a conscious awareness of you throughout his day. Grant him wisdom as he studies your Word, and let him rely fully on it. Let his heart beat in rhythm with yours. Keep him mindful of your promises and faithful to act on them. Help him to guard his thoughts so they will be honoring to you, edifying to others, and healthy for him. Encourage him with your approval. Honor his obedience as he humbles himself before you and submits himself to you. Keep him strong in his faith, grow his love for you, increase his desire to be close to you, and, in doing so, quench the fiery darts of the evil one.

You too, be patient and stand firm, because the Lord's coming is near. (James 5:8)

In everything, help him to stand firm, relying on the patience you give him as he grows ever more like your Son and lives as a man after your own heart.

My prayer is not that you take them out of the world but that you protect them from the evil one. (John 17:15)

Father, I lift up my husband to you and ask that you keep him close, protecting him physically, mentally, spiritually, and emotionally. While he lives in this world, he faces so many trials and temptations that would beat him down were it not for your faithful and abiding love. Help him to be aware of your love. Let him enjoy your love, experience your presence, participate in your peace, and glory in your grace. Reassure him that you are with him, you go before him, you surround him, and you have his back in every situation.

12

When He Is Overcome with Worry

Pray, and let God worry.
Martin Luther

"How'd you sleep last night?" This is pretty much my first question to Roger each morning.

"I didn't," Roger replied dully one day.

He didn't really need to tell me—I could see it in the bags under his eyes. Roger is not a great sleeper in the first place. There is a reason that our room is tricked out like the Stanford Sleep Disorders Clinic, with blackout shades, sound machines, and custom pillows, but lately Roger was sleeping less and feeling worse.

At this time, we were having huge money troubles. We felt sure that our decision to live on one income while I began pursuing writing and speaking full-time was directed by God.

But just because he was laying out our path didn't mean there weren't going to be a number of rather large potholes along the way.

One of my most annoying traits, according to Roger, is that no matter the circumstances, no matter which of our neighbors' kids are having a party while their folks are out of town, no matter what bills are piling up without the proper amount of income to match them, I can sleep. Not Roger. Now, he is about as mellow as they come. Almost nothing seems to faze him. But his brain takes all that anxiety, all that worry, all that stress, and channels it into not sleeping. That is why several times I have woken up in the middle of the night to Roger watching *Whose Line Is It Anyway?* reruns.

Not only does stress affect his sleep, it affects who he is. When Roger is overcome with worry, it's harder for him to feel confident in the decisions he is making. He starts to second-guess himself and compare himself to other men. Not a great place to be.

There is nothing harder for me as a wife than to see my husband wrapped up in worry and not be able to do anything about it. It has been just in the past few years of our marriage that I have recognized the effectiveness of prayer in making a real difference when it comes to worry in Roger's life—not just in the actual prayer, but also in his knowing that I'm praying for him. I really believe it gives Roger a different perspective on the things he is worrying over, helping him see them in the light of his relationship with Christ. When we truly understand how much God cares for us, it is easier to let go of worry as an unnecessary exercise in daily living.

I know that Roger is not alone. There are several different ways that men worry.

The Silent Worrier: My husband doesn't have hissy fits when he's worried. He's the silent worrier. He holds things in because he doesn't want to upset me. That may be because he knows I'm more emotional, but a godly man also wants to protect his wife, and part of that protection is handling things and not causing his wife fear.

Dawn

The Irritable Worrier: When my husband is worried, he's more irritable and short-tempered. He doesn't laugh as easily and seems preoccupied.

Linda

The Snapper: When my husband is worried, it's easy for his normally calm and cool demeanor to disappear and for him to start snapping at me or the kids. He usually doesn't get short with people outside the family. The good news is he recognizes it pretty quickly.

Marie

The Insomniac: During his difficult times, my husband will be more likely to get up very early, sometimes as early as three a.m. He's a freelance writer and web designer, so often he'll be found working during these times in his office at our house.

Melissa

The Circler: My husband will rant about other things until he finally circles around to what's bothering him.

Adina

Prayerfully Practical Steps

Like so many other areas of Roger's life, when I first recognized that he was worrying, I felt helpless to support him. But now I have a few things in my arsenal to help.

Recognize the Signs

Whatever type of worrier your husband is, he is probably giving off some sort of clue that he is feeling worried. It may be the fact that he seems a bit on edge or that your normally active husband is now planted in front of a *Deadliest Catch* marathon.

My prayer is that God would make me sensitive to what's going on in my husband's life. Most husbands are not going to come out and say, "Wow, I'm really worried about this problem at work." They are going to keep it to themselves, and then the stress will leak out in other ways. Ask God to help you recognize the signs.

God, I want to understand when my husband needs my compassion and love. Help me to be tenderhearted, sensitive to his needs, and kind, even when I don't feel like it.

Pray for the Burden

My first response in these situations is to think, *There is nothing I can do or say to help.* But then I remember the words of A. J. Gossip: "We can do nothing, we say sometimes, we can only pray. That, we feel, is a terribly precarious second best. So long as we can fuss and work and rush about, so long as we can lend a hand, we have some hope, but if we have to fall back upon God, ah, then things must be critical indeed!"[1] My prayers are not the last option when there is nothing else left; they are the first line of defense in protecting my husband.

In addition to praying, another antidote to worry is to remind my husband—and myself—of all his areas of strength. I need to live in the place of seeing not the problem but the resources God has already given my husband, just as Dawn does:

The key to helping my husband when he worries is to encourage him in his strengths—including strengths that I think might help him deal with the source of his worry—or simply to remind him that he is a capable man. This is part of my responsibility of respect (Eph. 5:33) for who he is.

Give Covert Care

I love the subtle ways that Linda works to help her husband cope with his chief worry:

> What worries him most often? Finances. That's his major responsibility, and he takes it very seriously. I view that responsibility as one of the ways he shows love to our family, so when it starts getting him stressed, I try to make sure I'm doing my part to ease his load. A note in his lunch, a favorite meal, sex to release the stress, keeping the kids busy, etc.

Linda isn't helping directly with the finances, but she is serving her husband in other ways to lighten the load where she can.

Make the Effort Known

Covert care is great, but there are times to let your husband know in no uncertain terms that you are on the same team:

> Recently my husband and his co-workers had to take a class and then take tests. Mind you, the tests were months after the class was completed. If they did not pass the tests, there was a chance that they could be fired from their jobs. The week preceding the tests, my husband became more closed off. He also became irritable around me and our children.
>
> To help him, I made sure that he had time to study for his test. I picked the kids up from day care, I took them with me on errands, and I even went to my mom's house for a bit so that he had total quiet in the house to study.

Vashie

Worry. It will kill you. Just ask the Israelites who got reports of the Promised Land's good and plenty but chose to listen to the naysayers who said there were BIG guys there who would eat them for lunch. The Israelites did not trust God and worried themselves to death. Literally. All the ones immobilized by worry and fear died in the desert before ever setting foot in the Promised Land. But had they listened to Joshua and Caleb, they would not have needed to be afraid, for God said he was with them and would lead and protect them. And that would have been enough.

This is what we need to remind our husbands of. God goes before them. He sees the path and clears it to make a safe way. When Gregg thinks about getting older, his parents' frailty, and his children's wanderings, he fears and worries. But that is the way of death. There is no joy in worry. I love how the Message phrases Philippians 4:6: "Let petitions and praises shape your worries into prayers, letting God know your concerns." Praising God is a surefire way to defuse worry and up the trust quotient. Here is my trust prayer:

Praying God's Word When He Worries

But he said to me, "My grace is sufficient for you, for my power is made perfect in weakness." Therefore I will boast all the more gladly about my weaknesses, so that Christ's power may rest on me. (2 Cor. 12:9)

Our dear and gracious Father, I come to you now on behalf of my husband. Lord, your Word tells us you are working through our weaknesses, so I ask that my husband would embrace your work rather than worry about his own shortcomings. It's so easy to see our own faults as just that: faults. Yet you, the Creator of the universe,

Your goodness is GREAT, Lord, for those who worship you. You have stored up goodness for my husband as he trusts in you (Ps. 31:19). You promise to strengthen him and to hold him up with your righteous arm (Isa. 41:10). But there are times when he is weak with worry. Worry immobilizes him, and he can't move to the right or the left because of fear. Cover him with your feathers and shield him with your wings from the harm of worry (Ps. 91:4). Gird him with truth that will act as his shield and battering ram. May the night not bring terror (Ps. 91:5), but when he lies down, may you bring him peace. Be his safe dwelling place (Ps. 4:8; Prov. 3:24). May he turn his worries into praises, remembering that you are his light and his salvation. Whom shall he fear (Ps. 27:1)? So be it!

Emily

care enough to turn each of our weaknesses into ways that we can brag about you. You are amazing!

This is my prayer for my husband—that when he looks at himself, he sees a reason to boast. May your power rest on him and guide him through this worry. Thank you, Jesus!

Keep your lives free from the love of money and be content with what you have, because God has said,
> "Never will I leave you;
> never will I forsake you." (Heb. 13:5)

God, why do we worry? I guess it's because we're human. I'm praying today for my husband, asking you to place the assurances of your Word in his heart. God, we know what it is to be in need, and we most certainly know what it is to have plenty. What I pray for myself, my husband, and my family is for us to be content. Contentment *means less worry! Hear my prayer and work in our hearts. Help my husband to know that you will never leave us or forsake us. Remind him that he is your child at all times and that as a loving parent, you will provide for all our needs.*

I thank you in advance for all you are going to do to provide for us as well as to calm our worries and fears. I love you!

Now to him who is able to do immeasurably more than all we ask or imagine, according to his power that is at work within us. (Eph. 3:20)

Lord, you are able to do immeasurably more than all we ask or imagine, according to your power that is at work within us. Amaze my husband today with your love and provision. Help him to see there is nothing he can worry about that you have not already handled on his behalf.

"For I know the plans I have for you," declares the LORD, "plans to prosper you and not to harm you, plans to give you hope and a future." (Jer. 29:11)

Wow, God! You have great plans for my husband. It's such a comfort knowing this. I pray that my husband will see those plans in action. Fill his heart with confidence in the big picture and the big plans you have designed for him.

There is no fear in love. But perfect love drives out fear. (1 John 4:18)

Help my husband to know that the perfect love you give drives out all fear and all worry. There is no worry in you. You guide his plans and replace fear with love. Thanks so much for being a God who cares, a God who plans, and a God who loves.

Cast all your anxiety on him because he cares for you. (1 Pet. 5:7)

As I watch my husband struggle over our bills and how to provide for us, I remember that you care deeply about him. Remind my husband that he is not alone in his concerns. Help him to turn to you when the stress gets heavy and he feels overwhelmed by his responsibilities. Show him how to roll his worries onto your strong shoulders, believing by faith that you will carry them in a way he cannot. Thank you for being our ultimate provider.

But blessed is the one who trusts in the Lord,
    whose confidence is in him.
They will be like a tree planted by the water
    that sends out its roots by the stream.
It does not fear when heat comes;
    its leaves are always green.
It has no worries in a year of drought
    and never fails to bear fruit. (Jer. 17:7–8)

Father, I know that it's more important to trust in you than ourselves. Help my husband place his confidence, his sure hope, in you so he won't worry. Show him where he might be trusting in his own abilities instead of your power, and root him deeply in your Word so he can stand strong. Establish his heart and mind in truth so he will bear lasting fruit for you in the days ahead.

For the Spirit God gave us does not make us timid, but gives us power, love and self-discipline. (2 Tim. 1:7)

There are many reasons to fear in our world today, and my husband may face many scary circumstances, but the worst fear of all is to think that he might not be right with you, Lord. That kind of fear is fueled by guilt, and it leads to a tormented spirit. I pray that my husband will fully know and rest in your great love. Give him joy in his spirit and freedom from all his fears and worries. Let him walk in the knowledge that he has power, love, and self-discipline and can accomplish anything because you give him these strengths.

Praise be to the God and Father of our Lord Jesus Christ, the Father of compassion and the God of all comfort, who comforts us in all our troubles, so that we can comfort those in any trouble with the comfort we ourselves receive from God. For just as we share abundantly in the sufferings of Christ, so also our comfort abounds through Christ. (2 Cor. 1:3–5)

There are times I just want to wrap my arms around my husband and make things better, Lord. I want to comfort him when life gets tough. But sometimes I don't have the words to say. His worries are too many and his hurt is just too deep. In those times, I pray that you will comfort him, encourage him, and assure him of your love. And then, after you meet his needs and give him a message of your faithfulness, I pray that you will give him opportunities to encourage others, helping them to sense your comfort and peace.

Call to me and I will answer you and tell you great and unsearchable things you do not know. (Jer. 33:3)

Life is far too complicated for us to have all the answers. We need wisdom, Father. When I think of my husband's responsibilities, especially in leading our home, I know he needs your guidance. Give him a spirit of discernment and understanding, and enable him to counter the enemy's temptation to worry. Help him call out to you each day, and give him the confidence that you will hear and answer. Speak clearly, Lord, so he won't miss your will, and give him a thankful heart to praise you for your wisdom.

Even to your old age and gray hairs
   I am he, I am he who will sustain you.
I have made you and I will carry you;
   I will sustain you and I will rescue you. (Isa. 46:4)

Father, I dream of growing old with my dear husband and enjoying the sunset of our years. But security is a fleeting thing. We can't know what lies ahead. Give my husband courage to face the future and trust you to supply every need. We don't need to worry because you are in control.

Do not be anxious about anything, but in every situation, by prayer and petition, with thanksgiving, present your requests to God. And the peace of God, which transcends all understanding, will guard your hearts and your minds in Christ Jesus. (Phil. 4:6–7)

Do not let my husband be anxious about anything, but in every situation, by prayer and petition, with thanksgiving, may he present his requests to you, O God. I pray that your peace, which transcends all understanding, will guard his heart and mind in Christ Jesus.

I lift up my eyes to the mountains—
   where does my help come from?
My help comes from the Lord,
   the Maker of heaven and earth. (Ps. 121:1–2)

Lord in heaven, please rescue my husband from his valley of worry and distress. Set his feet firmly on your mountaintop, where peace and joy abound. Remind him that you are there to help and comfort and guide. Shower him, I pray, with your loving presence. Calm and heal his heart, soul, and mind.

Therefore do not worry about tomorrow, for tomorrow will worry about itself. Each day has enough trouble of its own. (Matt. 6:34)

Help my husband face the challenges of each day without worry, knowing that he can turn to you for aid, comfort, and direction. Let him recognize the things he cannot change and let go of them. For the things he can change, allow him to feel your presence guiding him toward sound and right decisions. Give him a renewed spirit each day and a restful, peaceful sleep when night falls. When his burdens are heavy, remind him that your yoke is light and you can and will always carry him through difficult times.

13

His Past Mistakes

Prayer breaks all bars, dissolves all chains, opens
all prisons, and widens all straits by which God's
saints have been held.

E. M. Bounds

There may be things in your husband's past that he is not
proud of—whether it be past relationships, the use of drugs or
alcohol, addictions, or failing those he loved. Every man has a
past, and in that past there are things that he regrets. But God
is in the business of redemption—he loves taking broken lives
and making them whole again. He has no interest in your husband being weighed down by those past mistakes; God wants
him to experience new life through Jesus Christ, as David did:

> Back in the seventies, David sang and played guitar in night-
> clubs for a living before finally deciding to enroll at Georgia
> Tech in his early thirties. I'm sure you can envision the scene:
> alcohol, drugs, girls, and more girls.

He was married briefly and divorced. Several years later, he married the woman who is the mother of his children. Although he tried everything he could to keep the marriage together, Christ was not yet Lord of his life, and he could do nothing to convince his wife to stop her affairs. He endured yet another wrenching divorce. Stress took its toll, and at age forty-five, David suffered a heart attack. It was then that the doctors found out that his cholesterol was high and placed him on medication to control it.

Not long after that incident, as if that weren't horrific enough, David contracted pneumonia so deadly that he was placed in an induced coma for six days. No one thought he would pull through, but God had other plans. David's sister, a devout Christian, stayed with him for a month while he was recovering from the pneumonia. It was she who planted the seed of Christ in his heart, and there it has flourished to this day.

David will be the first to admit having made his fair share of mistakes in his life. Since we met and married in our early fifties, I did not live through these times with him, nor did he have to endure living through my own plethora of erroneous deeds, but we have readily confessed them to one another. We understand now, in looking back, what we could not see when going through these trials and tribulations: we were both trying to live out our lives without Christ at the center of them. Talk about a major mistake! We can both point to accepting him as our Lord and Savior as the crucial moment that both our lives were changed forever.

David has been able to leave his mistakes in his past and has allowed the lessons they taught him to have a positive impact on the present and in our relationship. He also sees how God has taken these former indiscretions and transformed them and him in mighty ways.

Marcy

Aren't we all hoping for that kind of ending? There is hope in Jesus Christ.

I know that some of you are reading this and thinking, *I wish his mistakes* were *in the past.* Maybe your husband is in rebellion right now. There is still hope.

One Sunday my pastor, Scott, asked that everyone in the congregation who had gone through some kind of rebellion at any point in their life stand up. About 75 percent of the room stood.

Next, he wanted to know how long the rebellion had lasted for each person:

"Less than a year? Sit down."

"Less than two years? Sit down."

"Less than three years? Sit down."

(This is when I sat down.)

"Less than five years? Sit down."

He went on and on like this until he said, "Less than ten years? Sit down."

At this point there were still a dozen people standing.

What I find remarkable is not that these people were in rebellion for so long. It's the fact that they were in rebellion for so long and were now standing here in a church, praising God. Think of all the family members and friends who represented those people standing. How many late-night prayers were said on their behalf? How much did others beg and plead with God because these people were living life without him? And now they were here. In church.

If your husband is still in rebellion, there is hope. Real hope in Jesus and real restoration.

Practical Steps

As we are praying for our husbands, there are some practical steps we can take to lessen the effects of those past mistakes on the men they are today.

Let them revisit the past, but don't be the one to take them there. I've seen so many women, including myself upon occasion, bring up the past to their husbands at the most inappropriate times. Dinner with another couple is not the time to bring up his drug history. He can bring it up, but you can't. It is up to him to determine who is safe and who isn't when it comes to sharing his past.

Encourage counseling. I think that every person, at some point in their life, is going to need someone on the outside to help them work through something. I recently had an acquaintance brag that she has never had to go to a counselor. All I could think was that she hadn't been honest enough with herself about when in her life she needed to see a counselor.

If your husband's past is haunting him, encourage counseling. If he refuses to go to it, go on your own.

Choose your words wisely. Mimi shared with me that she's changed the way she offers encouragement to her husband:

> I used to say, "Sweetie, I will be with you even if we lose everything." What I realized later was that the message he heard was, "I know you will blow it again and eventually we will lose everything, but I'll still be with you." I changed my response when he was discouraged to say, "I have confidence you will succeed. This burden will not own you because you are a child of Jesus, and he and I love you and know you can do anything if you include him."

Praying God's Word for His Past Mistakes

You will again obey the LORD and follow all his commands I am giving you today. Then the LORD your God will make you most prosperous in all the work of your hands and in the fruit of your womb, the young of your livestock and the crops of your land. The LORD will again delight in you and make you prosperous, just as he delighted in your ancestors, if you obey the LORD your God and keep his commands and decrees that are written in this Book of the Law and turn to the LORD your God with all your heart and with all your soul. (Deut. 30:8–10)

Father, my husband has sinned. He has failed to obey all your righteous commands and as a result has suffered both personally and financially. Thankfully, in his misery at the recognition of his failings, he has turned to you for mercy, which you so freely and generously give. And then, loving Savior, in your grace and kindness you do even more than that—you promise to renew, refresh, and restore him as he returns to your ways! Thank you, Father, for his repentance. Help him to fully embrace your forgiveness. Give him faith to believe you mean it when you say you will again delight in him and make his ways prosperous, that you will look on him with favor and bless him in every area of his life. Thank you for his sincere desire to please you. In his repentance, give him the ability to follow your ways, and renew the joy of his salvation.

And forgive us our debts,
    as we also have forgiven our debtors. (Matt. 6:12)

When something occurs that reminds my husband of past mistakes, please remind him in turn that they are exactly where they belong—in the past! Reassure him once again that all his sins were forgiven the moment he accepted you, dear Jesus, as his Savior. Surround him with your love and grace. Let him be at peace with what he cannot forget. Help him to do what is often the most difficult for each of us: forgive himself.

Because through Christ Jesus the law of the Spirit who gives life has set you free from the law of sin and death. (Rom. 8:2)

Help my husband not to dwell on the sins of his past. Let him know that while he wallowed in darkness, your plan to bring him to the light and to new life in you was even then at work. Allow him to view past stumbling blocks as stepping-stones that ultimately led him down the path to you. Continue to bless him and keep him in the law of the Spirit so he might do your will with joy and thanksgiving each day.

Therefore, there is now no condemnation for those who are in Christ Jesus. (Rom. 8:1)

Thank you for your grace and mercy reminding us that you do not condemn; you came to save. Help me to live out that truth as an example to my husband so he might realize that as your son, he does not have to live under the oppression of condemnation. That is the world's way—not yours!

"Come now, let us settle the matter,"
    says the LORD.
"Though your sins are like scarlet,
    they shall be as white as snow;
though they are red as crimson,
    they shall be like wool." (Isa. 1:18)

Thank you for the gift of the Holy Spirit that allows us to reason. Thank you that you love my husband light-years more than I do or can. Thank you that through the gift of your Son, Jesus Christ, you erased, blotted out, removed my beloved's past sins. You, O Lord, have restored him. Remind my husband that he is no longer bound by the sins that stained his life.

Therefore, if anyone is in Christ, the new creation has come: The old has gone, the new is here! (2 Cor. 5:17)

I am amazed, Jesus, at the magnitude of your love for my husband. Thank you for making him into the wonderful man he is. Thank you for taking his old self and his earthly attitudes and desires and replacing them with eternal values and character. Thank you for doing that every single day. For in you alone, my husband is becoming who you created him to be for me and for our marriage. You are so good.

The Lord our God is merciful and forgiving, even though we have rebelled against him. (Dan. 9:9)

I am so grateful to you for your willingness to forgive your errant children. I know that my husband has cried out to you in repentance for his rebellious spirit, and you, O Lord, have demonstrated your love for him by restoring him. Through your forgiveness and mercy, our marriage has grown stronger over these many years. Thank you, Father!

As far as the east is from the west,
>so far has he removed our transgressions from us.
>>(Ps. 103:12)

Father, this is a proclamation to me and to my husband to never hold on to our past grievances—the ones we have against one another or others. As you love my husband, Father, remind him that you have completely removed his past transgressions. Thank you, Lord, for your steadfastness toward the man you blessed my life with. Praise you!

14

Understanding God's Plan for His Life and Dreams

Prayer is weakness leaning on omnipotence.
W. S. Bowd

When your husband knows you are praying for God's plans for his life, he is more willing to pay attention to the nudging of the Holy Spirit. Life is a lot more interesting when a man is following the path God has for him.

His Dreams

I love this prayer that author Cindi McMenamin has in her book *When a Woman Inspires Her Husband*, about praying over his dreams:

God, thank You for the dreams You have placed within my husband's heart. Give me discernment that helps me to know which dreams are truly from You, and which ones are clearly not in his best interest. Give me a desire to help him experience all You want him to experience, and give me the ears to hear the dreams that work themselves up from his heart and out of his mouth. Help me to be affirming and encouraging in the presence of those dreams.

Lord, the word *encouragement* literally means "to put courage into," and that's what I want to do for my man when it comes to him pursuing and realizing the dreams You have placed in his heart. Help me to be his helper in the true sense of the word when it comes to drawing his dreams out of him, responding to him positively, encouraging him to take the next step, affirming his adventure, and making it happen for him—or trusting *You* to make it happen for him. When it comes to my husband's dreams, may I be the biggest cheerleader he has. And help me to realize that when he begins verbalizing what he longs for, what he's dreamed of, what he truly wishes or regrets, that I am on sacred ground and I must walk carefully to not damage or destroy anything You've put in Your precious son's heart.

Lord, give me the kind of heart for his dreams that *You* have for them.[2]

Praying God's Word for His Dreams

But seek first his kingdom and his righteousness, and all these things will be given to you as well. (Matt. 6:33)

Let my husband see you in everything he does. I pray that every desire he has comes from a desire to follow you. Lord, I pray he sees that every good thing comes from you.

But we have this treasure in jars of clay to show that this all-surpassing power is from God and not from us. (2 Cor. 4:7)

When my husband enjoys success in an endeavor, let him give you the honor and the glory. If he endures failure, may he pray to learn and understand your lesson for him. Remind him of your loving plan for his life. Help him to acknowledge that he has no power to accomplish things on his own; this is reserved for your infinite power alone. Let him be an open vessel, a jar of clay, through whom your living waters flow!

Comparing His Life to Others

Recently, Roger and I went out to dinner with a new couple, Jane and George. Jane and I have been friends for years, but this was the first time we were going out as couples—a huge step. Roger was having a great week—he had gotten some good feedback at his job, his kids were discussing college plans, and the website he created for me was getting some industry recognition. Our whole week had been a success, and I was looking forward to hanging out with our new friends.

Just a couple of minutes after sitting down to our bento boxes at a Japanese restaurant, the conversation turned to work. Who knew—Roger and George worked at the same huge tech company! What a coincidence.

As we started talking about balancing work with real life, it became clear that Jane and George were not from our hood. They definitely lived on the other side of the tracks—the "this is where the millionaires build their homes" side of the tracks. They had designed their home. And the cute little sports car George was driving? Let's just say he didn't get it from the same place that Roger and I bought our hand-me-down modes of transportation.

By no means were Jane and George bragging. The facts made themselves evident: we were dealing with people who had way more means than we did.

On the ride home, it became obvious that Roger was struggling.

"What's up, babe?" I asked. But I thought I already knew what was going on.

"Wow. It's just hard," Roger said. "We started our jobs within a year of each other, and look where we ended up. It's so hard to see someone who has been at the same place doing so much better than I am."

I wanted to point out to him that he had been a single dad for thirteen years, had done a great job supporting his kids, had provided private school for them, and was now taking care of them as well as a wife and two stepchildren. But there are just times when a wife needs to stop reasoning and start listening. I listened for the rest of the car ride home.

A few weeks later, Jane and I were out having coffee. As we talked about our dinner, Jane told me she had sensed that Roger got quieter as the night went on. I told Jane, in a very raw and honest moment, that Roger was struggling with comparing himself to George. (Jane is the kind of friend you can do that with.) And that's when I found out a little more about their situation.

Jane told me that George's family had money. Old money. That's how they were able to afford the property they built their house on. She also said that George struggled with many of the same issues as Roger when it came to his job—trying to feel successful in what he was doing in his job and his life.

I thought *I* was the one who spent all my time comparing myself to other people: "She's a better mother," or "I wish I could teach like she does; she's so spiritually deep," or "I wish I had her tiny waist." (Looking back on this list, I can see how perhaps my desires to be spiritually deep and have a tiny waist tell more about my insecurities than I really want it to.)

I really believed that my husband, in many ways, was beyond all the comparisons. He never talked about wanting to have the broad shoulders of another guy. It turns out his comparisons go deeper than that. He compares the kind of father he is to other dads at work and church. He compares the kind of success he has at work to other employees. He compares the kind of house he has to those of his brothers.

I am beginning to understand that every man does it, but nobody talks about it.

Praying God's Word When He Compares

But godliness with contentment is great gain. (1 Tim. 6:6)

Let my husband be content in the person you have made him to be. Assure him that your mighty hands are guiding him in all he does. Strengthen him in your Word and grant him your peace when challenges come. Allow him to see that true gain in life comes only from doing your will.

His Priorities

Every woman's magazine has some article dealing with women and their priorities. But men struggle with this just as much as we do.

Praying God's Word for His Priorities

For you are a people holy to the LORD your God. The LORD your God has chosen you out of all the peoples on the face of the earth to be his people, his treasured possession. (Deut. 7:6)

Thank you, God, that my husband is set apart and made holy by you. Help me to look at him as you do. Help him to feel how special and treasured he is. As he goes about his day, I pray that you would shine your love into his life.

My husband's biggest area of prayer need is being able to prioritize—remembering that God is always first and should have a fair amount of his time each day. Then we as his family would come next, receiving his time and attention as well. And not what is left over from the day, but the very best of him—meaning we don't want him to be grouchy and burnt-out when he gets home from work, but to be the kind, loving, and gentle husband and father God created him to be.

Although this sounds like a selfish prayer for us, really I mean it in his best interest, not ours. I think sometimes men are just so focused on what needs to be done next. They work hard to be good employees, good coaches (in our case), and good friends that sometimes they think, *Oh, there will always be time for those other things*, instead of realizing if God is first and family second, all those other things fall into place so much easier.

My other prayer for my husband often is for his time. Not only that he utilize it well (tying into the prayer for priorities) but that it be used to the fullest so he has time to accomplish all he needs to—so that he has time with God, good time with us, and plenty of time to be a good employee, a good coach, and a good friend.

Tina

Those who work their land will have abundant food,
but those who chase fantasies have no sense. (Prov. 12:11)

Thank you for my husband and the dreams you have placed in his heart. Thank you that he has visions and God-sized goals, that he can picture marvelous achievements and accomplishments. You have given him a mind with the ability to imagine and create. What

*a great gift! And yet in all that, Father, help him not to be satisfied
with only the vision. Give him the ability to translate those goals
into action, to recruit others to help him in the process, to do the
work required to bring those dreams to life. Help him to put legs
under the visions and not let them remain mere fantasies. Give him
endurance, perseverance, and the encouragement he needs to see
the process through to completion. And give him a great sense of
accomplishment for a job well done.*

If they obey and serve him,
> they will spend the rest of their days in prosperity
> and their years in contentment. (Job 36:11)

*Above all else, Father God, I pray that we would obey you. Help
my husband to follow your direction. Help him to serve you and to do
the things you want him to do. I pray the activities of his day would
be under your command and authority. Help him to submit to your
leadership knowing that the result will be blessings from you. Bring
him prosperity and contentment that come only from serving you.*

Moses said to the people, "Do not be afraid. Stand firm and
you will see the deliverance the LORD will bring you today. The
Egyptians you see today you will never see again. The LORD
will fight for you; you need only to be still." (Exod. 14:13–14)

*Give my husband eyes to see you, Lord. Let him know in the in-
nermost part of his heart that he does not stand alone. You are the
one fighting on his behalf.*

They replied, "Believe in the Lord Jesus, and you will be saved—
you and your household." (Acts 16:31)

*Believe! That is what you have called my husband to do. Yet often
he becomes fearful that your plan is for others and not necessarily
for him. He must believe to stand still and not fear. It is in believing
he will be able to see your rescue when it comes, and his belief will
strengthen the hearts of all our family. Lord, encourage his resolve
to believe in you.*

15

His Relationships
with Others

Therefore encourage one another and build each
other up, just as in fact you are doing.

1 Thessalonians 5:11

Besides his immediate family, your husband interacts with
dozens, if not hundreds, of people every week. When I asked
a handful of women what they were praying for in their husbands' lives, many of them said they were praying for other
godly men to come alongside their husbands.

I have spent large parts of my prayer time for Roger praying
for the other people in his life—his extended family, his co-
workers, his boss, and people he is serving alongside at church.

Growing up, and especially into my adult years, I saw my
brother Brian maintain a multitude of friends. Here we are
twenty years after high school graduation, and 90 percent of

his friends are still in his life. So I kinda thought there was something wrong with Roger when all he wanted to do was spend time with me and our kids.

I know that Roger has had good friends at various times in his life. But for him, simply working with other men in ministry or on the job is usually enough. Right now we have a high level of communication and accountability in our marriage, and at the moment, that seems to be sufficient for him. But I know there are men who want and need a group of guys to hold them accountable, talk through life, and pray through decisions.

When Your Husband Feels Alone

Author and speaker Mimi Moseley talks about a time in her marriage when her opportunities were growing, and her husband was feeling left behind.

> Marty was feeling that because of his job and travel, he could not meet with men to encourage and be encouraged. Instead of having men pour into his life, he took on the mantle of "pick yourself up by the bootstraps and get the job done," even if you get nothing in return. There was nothing I could do or say that would make him feel less alone.

Most men have a hard time admitting that they need others in their lives. Your husband may consider it a weakness to admit that.

> The second problem was that Marty was not seeking God for his worth, which caused him to actually repel the very men whom he desired to show him his value and affirm him.
>
> Marty would see what seemed to be success in other men and beat himself up that he wasn't them. A friend with a new car or someone with an air of having it all together

chipped away at him, adding to his view of himself as a provider failure. Even when some of these men's lives revealed trouble in their marriages, integrity, etc., he struggled to see the men as anything but good providers. He also found it difficult to be happy for a friend who closed a big deal or received a promotion.

Isolation combined with comparison is demoralizing. When any of us compares our inner lives with someone else's outer lives—our reality with the unrealistic perception of who the other person is—we will always come up lacking. We need to stay in Scripture and in prayer so we can have an accurate understanding of our worth in Christ.

Once Marty came to the end of himself, he found Jesus there with open arms and no judgment. Jesus called him to himself and showed Marty the value Jesus had for him. Immediately, men seemed to come out of the woodwork, affirming Marty (unsolicited) in his position as husband and father. Young men sought him out as a mentor for how to be the kind of godly man he was while working and being a dad.

Today, Marty has a ministry to many of the young men at our church. Our sons hear about how great their dad is from their friends. They in turn tell Marty, and Jesus continues to affirm him.

When Your Husband Has Trouble Connecting

As more and more men are working from home, their opportunity to connect becomes less and less likely.

When Marcus was taking summer school classes a number of years ago, I looked forward to the discussions we had when he got home in the evening. He'd tell me all about what he'd learned in class, and then we'd apply it to our jobs and parenting.

One day, however, he was strangely silent when he got home. Trying to spark our usual lively conversation, I asked, "So, how was class today?" I finally realized something was amiss when he replied flatly, "Fine," and left the room.

Later that evening, he started asking me questions. Each had four possible answers, and my goal was to identify the best one. I answered each question quickly, almost flippantly. After ten questions, he again left the room, looking more upset and sullen than before.

Days later, he finally told me that the questions he'd been asking were from an exercise they'd done in class that day—an EQ (emotional quotient) test. The highest score in class was an 8. Without even thinking, I'd gotten a 10.

Marcus, having poured agonizing thought into each question, scored a 1.

I stifled my "No duh!" reflex as I saw how deeply disturbed Marcus was by these results. He could not fathom how I could have scored so well with no effort. And he could not comprehend why his answers were supposedly "wrong," especially since he'd thought them through so carefully, so logically.

Until that day, Marcus had typically dismissed relational problems as "their fault"—someone else was always to blame, never him. This incident yanked that rug right out from under him, resulting in a profound sense of defectiveness. The recognition that he might be the common denominator in all of his difficult relationships left him feeling insecure and alienated.

Susan

The good news is that Susan is aware of this with Marcus, and instead of being stuck in blame, she knows how to pray for her husband and his relationships with others.

Praying God's Word for His Relationships

HIS REPUTATION

If I speak in the tongues of men or of angels, but do not have love, I am only a resounding gong or a clanging cymbal. (1 Cor. 13:1)

Thank you, Lord, for giving my husband a heart of love. Help him speak words of truth in love, not in judgment or criticism. Help him resist angry and damaging words. May all of his words bring life, healing, and help to others as he serves you.

For by the grace given me I say to every one of you: Do not think of yourself more highly than you ought, but rather think of yourself with sober judgment, in accordance with the faith God has distributed to each of you. For just as each of us has one body with many members, and these members do not all have the same function, so in Christ we, though many, form one body, and each member belongs to all the others. We have different gifts, according to the grace given to each of us. If your gift is prophesying, then prophesy in accordance with your faith; if it is serving, then serve; if it is teaching, then teach; if it is to encourage, then give encouragement; if it is giving, then give generously; if it is to lead, do it diligently; if it is to show mercy, do it cheerfully. (Rom. 12:3–8)

Thank you, Lord, for the talents and gifts that you have given my husband. Reveal to him the unique qualities of his God-given abilities. Show him where his gifts are needed in the body of Christ. Encourage him to submit to your will so he can serve in your power and strength.

His divine power has given us everything we need for a godly life through our knowledge of him who called us by his own glory and goodness. Through these he has given us his very great and precious promises, so that through them you may participate in the divine nature, having escaped the corruption in the world caused by evil desires.

For this very reason, make every effort to add to your faith goodness; and to goodness, knowledge; and to knowledge, self-control; and to self-control, perseverance; and to perseverance, godliness; and to godliness, mutual affection; and to mutual affection, love. (2 Pet. 1:3–7)

Thank you, Lord, for revealing your power and your promises to my husband. Provide the guidance he needs daily as he seeks your wisdom. Help him to persevere as he faces trouble in this world. Strengthen his body, soul, and spirit as he confesses and submits his areas of weakness to you.

Whoever would foster love covers over an offense,
> but whoever repeats the matter separates close friends.
> (Prov. 17:9)

Thank you, Lord, for giving my husband your gift of forgiveness. Help him overlook the offenses of others. Give him the desire to seek reconciliation when necessary. Bless him with the friendships he needs to grow in his faith.

Be merciful, just as your Father is merciful.
> Do not judge, and you will not be judged. Do not condemn, and you will not be condemned. Forgive, and you will be forgiven. Give, and it will be given to you. A good measure, pressed down, shaken together and running over, will be poured into your lap. For with the measure you use, it will be measured to you. (Luke 6:36–38)

Help my husband to be merciful to others around him. Help him not to judge or condemn them. Remind him that as he gives to others, so it will be given to him.

You are judging by appearances. If anyone is confident that they belong to Christ, they should consider again that we belong to Christ just as much as they do. So even if I boast somewhat freely about the authority the Lord gave us for building you up rather than tearing you down, I will not be ashamed of it.

I do not want to seem to be trying to frighten you with my letters. . . .

We do not dare to classify or compare ourselves with some who commend themselves. When they measure themselves by themselves and compare themselves with themselves, they are not wise. We, however, will not boast beyond proper limits, but will confine our boasting to the sphere of service God himself has assigned to us, a sphere that also includes you. (2 Cor. 10:7–9, 12–13)

Help my husband refrain from judging others by reminding him that they have just as much value as he does. Help him to refrain from boastful words that only build up and edify himself. Instead may he boast in you and give you all the credit for the work you're doing in him. Help him to encourage others in the work they're doing for you. I pray that those around him, including myself, will be faithful in lifting up my husband, encouraging him to move forward on your path and in the direction you're taking him.

With His Co-workers

Slaves, obey your earthly masters in everything; and do it, not only when their eye is on you and to curry their favor, but with sincerity of heart and reverence for the Lord. Whatever you do, work at it with all your heart, as working for the Lord, not for human masters, since you know that you will receive an inheritance from the Lord as a reward. It is the Lord Christ you are serving. (Col. 3:22–24)

Remind my husband today that the work he is doing is for you, Lord. That you provided this job for him and you have a plan and a purpose for him in doing it. Help him to develop a good relationship with co-workers as well as those in authority over him.

The centurion replied, "Lord, I do not deserve to have you come under my roof. But just say the word, and my servant will be healed. For I myself am a man under authority, with soldiers under me. I tell this one, 'Go,' and he goes; and that one, 'Come,' and he comes. I say to my servant, 'Do this,' and he does it."

When Jesus heard this, he was amazed and said to those following him, "Truly I tell you, I have not found anyone in Israel with such great faith." (Matt. 8:8–10)

I pray that you will help my husband, an overseer of the employees, to exhibit his faith in you. May your light shine out of him in the way he treats those around him. Help him to have compassion toward his co-workers and the faith the centurion did.

These, then, are the things you should teach. Encourage and rebuke with all authority. Do not let anyone despise you. (Titus 2:15)

I come to you today, Lord, asking that you be with my husband. His job gives him authority over others; I ask that you will fill him with your words and actions so he can encourage those who work under him. Help him as he's correcting their work to treat them with respect and dignity. I pray that those who work for him will not despise him or be disrespectful toward him.

With Other Men

You, however, must teach what is appropriate to sound doctrine. Teach the older men to be temperate, worthy of respect, self-controlled, and sound in faith, in love and in endurance. . . .

Similarly, encourage the young men to be self-controlled. In everything set them an example by doing what is good. In your teaching show integrity, seriousness and soundness of speech that cannot be condemned, so that those who oppose you may be ashamed because they have nothing bad to say about us.

Teach slaves to be subject to their masters in everything, to try to please them, not to talk back to them, and not to steal from them, but to show that they can be fully trusted, so that in every way they will make the teaching about God our Savior attractive.

For the grace of God has appeared that offers salvation to all people. It teaches us to say "No" to ungodliness and worldly passions, and to live self-controlled, upright and godly lives in this present age, while we wait for the blessed hope—the appearing of the glory of our great God and Savior, Jesus Christ, who gave himself for us to redeem us from all wickedness and to purify for himself a people that are his very own, eager to do what is good. (Titus 2:1–2, 6–14)

You, God, have established relationships for a reason. Remind my husband that his relationships with other men are very important. Remind him that he can lift them up by encouraging them and rebuke those who are doing wrong. My husband can easily neglect friendships and meeting with friends because he is faithful to the demands of providing for our family. Remind him not to neglect meeting with other men, sharing with them, and taking the advice they're willing to offer to help him in his own life.

Live such good lives among the pagans that, though they accuse you of doing wrong, they may see your good deeds and glorify God on the day he visits us.

Submit yourselves for the Lord's sake to every human authority: whether to the emperor, as the supreme authority, or to governors, who are sent by him to punish those who do wrong and to commend those who do right. (1 Pet. 2:12–14)

Help my husband to be a godly example to everyone he encounters. Help him to be an example to the bosses above him at work, his other co-workers, his friends, and his family. Let your light shine through him for all the world to see so others too can glorify you.

But as for you, continue in what you have learned and have become convinced of, because you know those from whom you learned it, and how from infancy you have known the Holy Scriptures, which are able to make you wise for salvation through faith in Christ Jesus. All Scripture is God-breathed and is useful for teaching, rebuking, correcting and training in righteousness, so that the servant of God may be thoroughly equipped for every good work. (2 Tim. 3:14–17)

Thank you, Lord, for guiding and directing my husband from his early days of life. Help him to share with others the things you have taught him through all those years. Be with him as he instructs other men in your ways. Guide him as he shares with others about your gift of salvation to the world. Help those who hear his words and see his actions turn from their old ways and turn to you, Jesus.

As God's co-workers we urge you not to receive God's grace in vain. For he says,

"In the time of my favor I heard you,
   and in the day of salvation I helped you."
I tell you, now is the time of God's favor, now is the day of salvation.

We put no stumbling block in anyone's path, so that our ministry will not be discredited. Rather, as servants of God we commend ourselves in every way: in great endurance; in troubles, hardships and distresses; in beatings, imprisonments and riots; in hard work, sleepless nights and hunger; in purity, understanding, patience and kindness; in the Holy Spirit and in sincere love; in truthful speech and in the power of God; with weapons of righteousness in the right hand and in the left; through glory and dishonor, bad report and good report; genuine, yet regarded as impostors; known, yet regarded as unknown; dying, and yet we live on; beaten, and yet not killed; sorrowful, yet always rejoicing; poor, yet making many rich; having nothing, and yet possessing everything.

We have spoken freely to you, Corinthians, and opened wide our hearts to you. We are not withholding our affection from you, but you are withholding yours from us. As a fair exchange—I speak as to my children—open wide your hearts also. (2 Cor. 6:1–13)

Lord, help my husband not to take your grace in vain. Help him accept it and be full of grace toward others, just as you are toward us. Help my husband and other men to be truthful in their words and full of genuine love toward one another. Help my husband to stand strong if anyone mistreats him in any way and to turn the trials and persecution over to you. May my husband and the other men in his life have hearts open to you, encouraging each other in situations that arise in their lives by turning to you and trusting you completely.

In Church

They preached the gospel in that city and won a large number of disciples. Then they returned to Lystra, Iconium and Antioch, strengthening the disciples and encouraging them to remain true to the faith. "We must go through many hardships to enter the kingdom of God," they said. Paul and Barnabas appointed elders for them in each church and, with prayer and fasting, committed them to the Lord, in whom they had put their trust. (Acts 14:21–23)

Help my husband, spiritual leaders, and elders of our church, dear Lord, to encourage the congregation and each other to stay faithful to good works for you and your kingdom. May they remind each other of your faithfulness and help each other through the trials and hardships that we all face. Help each of us to put our trust in you in everything.

And let us consider how we may spur one another on toward love and good deeds, not giving up meeting together, as some are in the habit of doing, but encouraging one another—and all the more as you see the Day approaching. (Heb. 10:24–25)

Encourage my husband in his relationships with those he works with in service to you, Lord. May he help others to do the good works you have called them to do by lifting them up with supporting words and prayers.

Have confidence in your leaders and submit to their authority, because they keep watch over you as those who must give an account. Do this so that their work will be a joy, not a burden, for that would be of no benefit to you. (Heb. 13:17)

I pray that you will help my husband to respect and submit to the leaders of our church. Remind him that you hold everyone accountable for their work with your church and all that happens there. Help my husband to give any issues he has to you as the true authority. Help him to be a joy to his fellow workers in the mission of your church and to find his place in the work you have called him to do there.

16

His Relationship
with You

Our prayer must not be self-centered. It must arise
not only because we feel our own need as a burden
we must lay upon God, but also because we are so
bound up in love for our fellow men that we feel their
need as acutely as our own. To make intercession
for men is the most powerful and practical way in
which we can express our love for them.

John Calvin

For many of you, this is the whole reason you picked up the
book. Perhaps you even skipped to this chapter first. I understand. While we are here on earth, we will derive a lot of pleasure—or pain—from this one relationship, our marriage. So
it makes a lot of sense to spend a good portion of our prayer
time covering it.

When things are going well, there is nothing better than being in love with the man you have committed your life to. When you agree on finances, plans, and what to have for dinner, there is almost nothing better than the safety and security of going through life with someone you love.

But when life is stressful, there is no place the stress shows up faster than in your marriage. And that is just plain painful. I know when I get overwhelmed, stressed out, or scared, Roger is the one I naturally take those feelings out on. I don't mean to—really! But he is usually the one standing closest to me when things explode, and he takes the brunt of the hit. One of the things I need to remember in that situation is that God did not intend for my husband to become my emotional dumping ground. God wants us to bring every worry, every anxiety, every problem, every sin to him.

I want you to be encouraged. I want you to know that you are already doing more for your marriage by committing to pray for him than most wives will ever do for their husbands. Just the simple act of praying for your husband and asking for God's direction is a huge step in having a better relationship with your man.

When I dropped the agenda I had in praying for Roger (though not without a lot of conviction and soul wrestling), I had a new freedom in my prayer life. It wasn't up to me to change Roger into the kind of husband I wanted. God started to show both of us that we needed to stop looking to each other to meet all of our needs and start looking to our Creator to meet them. It took a lot of the pressure off Roger—and off me.

Practical Steps

Along with my prayers, I also need to make sure that my words to my husband show him that we are on the same team.

I love how Ronnie discovered this simple (but not easy) truth in her relationship with her husband:

> Several years ago I went to our pastor to tell him that my husband was short-tempered and angry at home. Any little thing would cause him to fly off the handle. Truthfully, what I was hoping for was an ally who would go to my husband and tell him that his sweet wife and adorable, innocent children deserved to be treated better than that. Instead, the pastor asked me, "Is there anything in his life right now that is overwhelming—work, maybe? When I have too much on my plate or a difficult situation that's really bothering me, it's really hard for me to be kind and considerate at home."
>
> As I thought about what he said, I realized that my husband was under a tremendous amount of pressure at work. He was working long hours, had a heavy deadline coming up, and didn't feel like he had the support of his peers at the time.
>
> Suddenly, instead of feeling angry and needing to "fix" his bad behavior, I felt tremendous compassion for him and the burden he was bearing. I went home with a completely different attitude. Instead of waiting like a goalie, prepared to defend the rest of us against his moods, I switched teams and put his jersey back on. As his teammate, I started asking him, "What can I do for you today to help you?" and "How can I pray for you tomorrow while you're at work?" I also made the time to sit and listen to him so he could talk about everything that was going on. Or, if he didn't want to talk, I respected that and prayed for him again (and again and again).
>
> In only one day, he was acting more like his normal self.
>
> Now anytime his fuse seems shorter than normal, I start by asking or looking at how things are going with work or school. Acting as his loving helper instead of his opponent has really defused the situation time and time again.

So how do we practically and prayerfully let our husbands know that we are on the same team? I think the biggest thing we can do is to speak well of them, and about them, in every situation.

Always speak to him respectfully, even while vehemently disagreeing with him. You absolutely should hold your own values and opinions in your marriage. A good disagreement is good for a marriage. However, it is never, ever okay to be disrespectful to your husband. Not even when he is disrespectful. Not even when he has made a huge mistake. Never.

Always honor him in front of your kids. When you disrespect their dad, you are killing a little bit of your children.

Always honor him in front of others. Your friends, his mother—it doesn't matter. The only gossip that should be coming out of your mouth is about how awesome he is. If you need to speak about your husband to someone (and in every marriage there is a time for that), then a counselor is the one to go to.

Praying God's Word for His Relationship with You

Do two walk together
    unless they have agreed to do so? (Amos 3:3)

Lord, guide and guard our wills so our steps in our marriage journey may be in tandem. Open our eyes and hearts to one another when challenges and obstacles present detours along the road we strive to follow together. When we falter or fall along the way, let us offer a comforting hand to each other. Help us at all times to discern the direction you would have us take.

Make every effort to live in peace with everyone and to be holy; without holiness no one will see the Lord. See to it that no one falls short of the grace of God and that no bitter root grows up to cause trouble and defile many. (Heb. 12:14–15)

Sanctify our relationship with your holy presence, that we might be for each other a blessed oasis in a dry and desert land. Help us to resolve disagreements and hurts gently, with love, patience, and abiding respect, so that neither bitterness nor resentment will ever take root in our hearts. Let the divine light of your love so shine through our marriage that we present a holy example to others and lead them to your truth.

Do you see someone who speaks in haste?
There is more hope for a fool than for them. (Prov. 29:20)

When we are dissatisfied, disgruntled, or disappointed, help us to stop and reflect about the reasons before blurting out hasty accusations at one another. Let us always measure our words before we speak; let them be a balm and never a barb. Infuse us with your grace, and remind us, even when we least want to hear it, that we love each other because you loved us first. May that thought soften our hearts and curtail our tongues.

And now these three remain: faith, hope and love. But the greatest of these is love. (1 Cor. 13:13)

You have founded our marriage on the firm trinity of faith, hope, and love. Continue to bless us, Lord, that we may always share faith in you and in each other, hope in your promised salvation and for our future together, and a boundless love for you and the precious promises you have given us.

Therefore if you have any encouragement from being united with Christ, if any comfort from his love, if any common sharing in the Spirit, if any tenderness and compassion, then make my joy complete by being like-minded, having the same love, being one in spirit and of one mind. Do nothing out of selfish ambition or vain conceit. Rather, in humility value others above yourselves, not looking to your own interests but each of you to the interests of the others.

In your relationships with one another, have the same mind-set as Christ Jesus. (Phil. 2:1–5)

Not only does it give you joy, Lord, when my husband and I are of one mind in the decisions we make, but it also fills both my husband and me with joy. Help us each day to submit to your instructions for us, then allow us to come together in unity in making wise choices for our family. Help us to remove any selfish ambitions and to make each other's interests and needs more important than our own.

We who are strong ought to bear with the failings of the weak and not to please ourselves. Each of us should please our neighbors for their good, to build them up. For even Christ did not please himself but, as it is written: "The insults of those who insult you have fallen on me." For everything that was written in the past was written to teach us, so that through the endurance taught in the Scriptures and the encouragement they provide we might have hope.

May the God who gives endurance and encouragement give you the same attitude of mind toward each other that Christ Jesus had, so that with one mind and one voice you may glorify the God and Father of our Lord Jesus Christ.

Accept one another, then, just as Christ accepted you, in order to bring praise to God. (Rom. 15:1–7)

I pray, Lord, that you help my husband and me to encourage each other so we can have hope in all circumstances. Father, teach me to bear with those weak things in my husband and not look only to please myself. I pray that we would build each other up. Thank you for your Word that teaches us about endurance and gives us hope. Teach us to be one mind and one voice in all areas of our marriage.

Finally, all of you, be like-minded, be sympathetic, love one another, be compassionate and humble. (1 Pet. 3:8)

It is so easy not to humble ourselves. Lord, both my husband and I need your help in being humble and compassionate toward each other. Join us together to be like-minded, sympathetic, and loving in all areas of our marriage. We turn to you for your help and support.

The LORD God said, "It is not good for the man to be alone. I will make a helper suitable for him." . . .

The man said,

"This is now bone of my bones
and flesh of my flesh;
she shall be called 'woman,'
for she was taken out of man."

That is why a man leaves his father and mother and is united to his wife, and they become one flesh. (Gen. 2:18, 23–24)

Father, you created relationships. The most important in each of our lives is a relationship with you, then with others. You created marriages for us to have a helper and companion. Thank you so much for this design and for the companion you gave me in this life. Help us as we're learning to become "one flesh," as you say we are to be in your Word. Help us to be of one mind, supporting each other without reserve for all the years to come.

Therefore, my dear friends, as you have always obeyed—not only in my presence, but now much more in my absence—continue to work out your salvation with fear and trembling, for it is God who works in you to will and to act in order to fulfill his good purpose.

Do everything without grumbling or arguing, so that you may become blameless and pure, "children of God without fault in a warped and crooked generation." Then you will shine among them like stars in the sky as you hold firmly to the word of life. And then I will be able to boast on the day of Christ that I did not run or labor in vain. But even if I am being poured out like a drink offering on the sacrifice and service coming from your faith, I am glad and rejoice with all of you. So you too should be glad and rejoice with me. (Phil. 2:12–18)

Help my husband and me to keep from grumbling and arguing with each other. Help us to treat each other with respect and always strive to be more and more one-minded in our relationship. May we become like stars by shining your light through our marriage, so when we gather with others, they will see you and your involvement in our marriage.

Wives, in the same way submit yourselves to your own husbands so that, if any of them do not believe the word, they may be won over without words by the behavior of their wives, when they see the purity and reverence of your lives. Your beauty should not come from outward adornment, such as elaborate hairstyles and the wearing of gold jewelry or fine clothes. Rather, it should be that of your inner self, the unfading beauty of a gentle and quiet spirit, which is of great worth in God's sight. For this is the way the holy women of the past who put their hope in God used to adorn themselves. They submitted themselves to their own husbands, like Sarah, who obeyed Abraham and called him her lord. You are her daughters if you do what is right and do not give way to fear. (1 Pet. 3:1–6)

Help me, Lord, to be ever mindful of showing respect for my husband—not only around other people but also when we're home alone. Help me to be as concerned with my attitude and behavior as I am with how I look. Help me to have a gentle, quiet spirit with my husband that lifts him up and shows him his worth to me.

Her husband is respected at the city gate,
    where he takes his seat among the elders of the land.
    (Prov. 31:23)

Lord, I love you and trust you. I ask for your grace and help in being a busy, helpful, loving companion for my husband, treating him with honor and respect. By doing this, he will find himself respected in the areas of work you have called him to. Help me to be ever mindful of his reputation and helpful to my husband in this way.

However, each one of you also must love his wife as he loves himself, and the wife must respect her husband. (Eph. 5:33)

I could use your help, Lord, to shower my husband with the love and respect he deserves from me. Help me to be the wife he needs, and likewise, help my husband to be the husband I need.

In the same way, the women are to be worthy of respect, not malicious talkers but temperate and trustworthy in everything. (1 Tim. 3:11)

Help me to keep silent and not gossip about others. Help me to have an even temperament and not be easily offended or angered. I pray, dear Lord, that others—and most importantly, my husband—find me trustworthy.

But I want you to realize that the head of every man is Christ, and the head of the woman is man, and the head of Christ is God. . . .

Nevertheless, in the Lord woman is not independent of man, nor is man independent of woman. For as woman came from man, so also man is born of woman. But everything comes from God. (1 Cor. 11:3, 11–12)

Father, you are the head of our family and the head of our marriage. You have a divine order for marriages and relationships. Help us to remember this order and not try to assert our own way, disrupting what you have designed.

Submit to one another out of reverence for Christ.

Wives, submit yourselves to your own husbands as you do to the Lord. For the husband is the head of the wife as Christ is the head of the church, his body, of which he is the Savior. Now as the church submits to Christ, so also wives should submit to their husbands in everything.

Husbands, love your wives, just as Christ loved the church and gave himself up for her to make her holy, cleansing her by the washing with water through the word, and to present her to himself as a radiant church, without stain or wrinkle or any other blemish, but holy and blameless. In this same way, husbands ought to love their wives as their own bodies. He who loves his wife loves himself. After all, no one ever hated their own body, but they feed and care for their body, just as Christ does the church—for we are members of his body. "For this reason a man will leave his father and mother and be united to his wife, and the two will become one flesh." This is a profound mystery—but I am talking about Christ and the church. However, each one of you also must love his wife as he loves himself, and the wife must respect her husband. (Eph. 5:21–33)

Help my husband and me to meditate on and live out this divine order you created. Help me to be the wife my husband desires and to find out which needs of his I can fill. I also pray for my husband to seek out and learn all that I need from him. Give us a love for each other that honors you.

But since sexual immorality is occurring, each man should have sexual relations with his own wife, and each woman with her own husband. The husband should fulfill his marital duty to his wife, and likewise the wife to her husband. The wife does not have authority over her own body but yields it to her husband. In the same way, the husband does not have authority over his own body but yields it to his wife. Do not deprive each other except perhaps by mutual consent and for a time, so that you may devote yourselves to prayer. Then come together again so that Satan will not tempt you because of your lack of self-control. (1 Cor. 7:2–5)

Father, I pray that in this world where sex is seen as cheap, my husband and I would value it as one of your greatest gifts. Bring us together in every aspect of our marriage. I pray that our marriage would be free of selfishness and honor each other in all that we do. I pray that we would have eyes only for each other.

I am my beloved's and my beloved is mine;
he browses among the lilies. (Song of Sol. 6:3)

Father, I pray that my husband and I would always be of one mind in every area of our marriage. May my husband walk through life secure in our marriage, never doubting my love or faithfulness.

17

His Parenting

My father used to play with my brother and me in the yard. Mother would come out and say, "You're tearing up the grass." "We're not raising grass," Dad would reply. "We're raising boys."

Harmon Killebrew

The world isn't kind to fathers. Every dad has hopes and plans for his family, but many dads feel unsure and incapable of being the kind of father their children need. The area where my husband has had the most self-doubt and insecurity is parenting. This, I must say, completely blows my mind. Roger loves his kids and has been a great dad and stepdad. I've watched Roger—who has spent a total of about ten hours of his life watching professional sports—raise a son who loves nothing more than to play hockey, run track, and participate in basically any sport available to him. I've watched him—a man who was raised in a household with three boys—navigate the murky waters of raising a teenage girl. I've also watched Roger—who often felt overwhelmed by his own two kids—bring two stepkids into his home and learn how to be a good man in their life without trying to be their father.

Roger has two kids who love, respect, and want to hang out with him, as well as two stepkids who think he is smart, fun, and reliable, and yet he still doubts himself. All he can see are the times that he was less than perfect while parenting.

It's in parenting that each of us can see our own insecurities and failings magnified. Oh, and if your kids are past the age of ten, it's easy for them to sniff out self-doubt and use it to their advantage.

I hesitate to put labels on our husbands' behaviors. Would we want our husbands to label our actions? One man's idea of organized is another man's idea of a control freak. But I've heard from enough women who were concerned about their husbands' approach to parenting that I thought it would be valuable to include some prayers on the subject.

My warning, however, is this: just because your husband has a different temperament when it comes to parenting doesn't mean it needs to be changed.

Feeling Inadequate as a Father

I'd been at church for a few hours before the first service was to start, helping out with the rehearsal, getting kids into child care, etc. One of my friends, Katie, who is a gifted vocalist, was rehearsing a solo with the band. She had brought her daughter, Lindsay, with her to play with the other kiddos, but her husband, Lee, and their newborn, Erik, were sleeping in at home to come later to the service. Just as the first service began, Lee came strolling through the doors, saying hi to friends and ready to head off to the sanctuary. But something was wrong. . . .

"Um, Lee," I asked, "where's Erik?"

With only three words—"Don't tell Katie!"—Lee turned around and bolted for the parking lot. Forty minutes later he returned with Erik, who had still been sound asleep in his crib when Lee burst through the front door of his home.

An honest slipup can stick with us for years. It's good to know that we don't have to be perfect parents. God can fill in the holes where our skills and knowledge are lacking.

I am so grateful for the following passage of Scripture:

> Every year Jesus' parents went to Jerusalem for the Festival of the Passover. When he was twelve years old, they went up to the festival, according to the custom. After the festival was over, while his parents were returning home, the boy Jesus stayed behind in Jerusalem, but they were unaware of it. Thinking he was in their company, they traveled on for a day. Then they began looking for him among their relatives and friends. When they did not find him, they went back to Jerusalem to look for him. After three days they found him in the temple courts, sitting among the teachers, listening to them and asking them questions. Everyone who heard him was amazed at his understanding and his answers. When his parents saw him, they were astonished. His mother said to him, "Son, why have you treated us like this? Your father and I have been anxiously searching for you."
>
> "Why were you searching for me?" he asked. "Didn't you know I had to be in my Father's house?" But they did not understand what he was saying to them.
>
> Then he went down to Nazareth with them and was obedient to them. But his mother treasured all these things in her heart. And Jesus grew in wisdom and stature, and in favor with God and man. (Luke 2:41–52)

Mary and Joseph lost Jesus. And not just "I turned around for a second at Target and he was hiding behind the display of socks" kind of lost. We're talking days of him being missing. If that had happened today, Child Protective Services would have been knocking on Joseph and Mary's door when they got home. So if perfect parents were not required to raise the Son of God, why do we demand perfect parenting for our spouses and ourselves?

Recently my friend Robin was sitting in a church service as her pastor said, "What if God only did in my home what I prayed for?" That's how I need to remember to pray for my family—as if God would do in my home only what I prayed for.

Praying God's Word for His Parenting

A foolish child is a father's ruin,
    and a quarrelsome wife is like
    the constant dripping of a leaky roof. (Prov. 19:13)

Today, Father, help me remember that while my husband is not a perfect parent, neither am I. When I am tempted to "rescue" our children from him, remind me that I don't want to be as annoying—and ultimately as damaging—as a dripping, leaky roof. Help me teach our children to respect their father through my honoring of him as my partner in parenting.

Only be careful, and watch yourselves closely so that you do not forget the things your eyes have seen or let them fade from your heart as long as you live. Teach them to your children and to their children after them. Remember the day you stood before the LORD your God at Horeb, when he said to me, "Assemble the people before me to hear my words so that they may learn to revere me as long as they live in the land and may teach them to their children." (Deut. 4:9–10)

I pray for my husband's parenting, but I also pray for his character, which greatly affects his parenting. In our bathroom we have a chart that I printed from a blog awhile back. It's titled "Praying for Your Children." Each day has a Scripture to pray for your child—just one verse pertaining to characteristics we all as parents want our children to embrace. As we pray these over our kids, I've also taken to praying them over my husband—that he will embrace these not only for himself but also so that he can model them for our children and others. As a pastor, he has a burden to be an example to those around him, and I know that at times he feels the pressure of that responsibility. So each day as I pray over my children (while brushing my teeth, usually), I also include him in those character prayers.

Amy

I pray that my dear husband will be careful and watch himself closely so that he doesn't forget the things he has seen. May he pass on to his children and grandchildren how God has worked in his life, has helped him become who he is in Christ today, and has changed him completely. I pray that he will gather his family each day to break the bread of life with them and teach them how to reverence and fear the Lord. I pray that he will be sensitive to your Spirit so our children will take heed of his commitment to you.

Start children off on the way they should go,
> and even when they are old they will not turn from it.
> (Prov. 22:6)

I pray that you would help my husband be a wise parent while the kids are still at home. Even though we both fail over and over as parents, I pray that you will strengthen us as we strive not only to teach our kids your laws but to live them out ourselves.

Fix these words of mine in your hearts and minds; tie them as symbols on your hands and bind them on your foreheads. Teach them to your children, talking about them when you sit at home and when you walk along the road, when you lie down and when you get up. (Deut. 11:18–19)

You say, Lord, for us to fix your words into our hearts and minds, to tie them as symbols on our hands and on our foreheads, and to teach them to our children when we're in our home, when we're walking along the road, and when we lie down and get up. Dear Lord, as a wife and mother, I am lifting up my husband in prayer. May your Spirit remind him, as head of our home, to take the lead by teaching his children and family your ways. I pray that he will take the time to study and pray with us every day. I pray that he will desire to be a godly example to his family, and that you will remind him daily to take his role seriously as the head of our home.

One of the hardest things as a mom is to see bitterness and strife between your husband and your kids:

Tony is the youngest child by twenty years, born when his father—a strict authoritarian—was in his mid-fifties, with high expectations and little patience. His primary mode of relating to Tony as a child was to bombard him with factual questions about topics he (Tony's father) had been reading. If Tony could not answer or answered incorrectly, his father would sigh with disappointment and tell him to be sure to have the right answer the next time he was asked.

As a result, Tony is hyper-focused on appearing intelligent and all-knowing. He puts enormous effort into always being right and making sure it's impossible for him to be wrong. The two primary ways of triggering his anger (which is how he, like many men, expresses fear) are to question his judgment and to doubt his intelligence.

Parenting complicates his life greatly, as both of our children are strong-willed individuals who love to question, doubt, argue, and just plain tease for the sake of being ornery. They love nothing more than to catch their father in an error and then remind him of it as frequently as possible. This becomes a vicious cycle, as he reasserts his all-knowing father status and they try to pester him out of his perfectionism.

Tony desperately needed his father to say to him, "You are my beloved son, in whom I am well pleased!" And his children need to hear that he loves them, in spite of their myriad imperfections and failures to live up to his sky-high standards.

Abby

Fathers, do not embitter your children, or they will become discouraged. (Col. 3:21)

Here I am, Lord, again praying for the relationship between my husband and our kids. You instruct fathers not to exasperate their children. However, not only are they exasperated, but so am I. Dear Lord, I pray that you will help my husband to see how his words and actions are reflecting on our kids. I also pray that his eyes and heart will be open to hearing the echo of the same words his parents said to him when he was young and how he felt at that time. Give him clarity on how he needs to treat our kids and talk to them in ways that honor you. Give him a contrite spirit and the ability to humble himself for their sakes and mine so that there can be healing in all our relationships. Thank you, Lord, for answering my prayer.

Here is another prayer for that verse:

I pray this man's heart pauses to remember he too was once a child with fears and discouragements. Grant him the innocence he once had as he responds to our children. Help him to walk in those shoes again, and give him the power to correct with love just as you discipline those you love.

Fathers, do not provoke your children to anger, but bring them up in the discipline and instruction of the Lord. (Eph. 6:4 NASB)

Dear Lord, please help my husband to see clearly how his actions and words have been instrumental in our children's anger. Help him to see their viewpoint, and soften his resolve to always be right. Help him to stop trying to control everyone's thoughts and actions to the point that we all feel suffocated and put down. Help him to care about what the other members of our family are experiencing and understand that not everything is all about him.

As women, it's so easy to take charge in the parenting roll. It just feels natural since we are usually the primary caregivers. But it's important for our kids to see that wives and husbands are a team in every respect of parenthood.

I give my husband and his parenting wisdom a great deal of credit for the success of our twenty-eight-year marriage; in fact, it contributed to our getting married in the first place!

Jim's first wife had died, leaving him with a five-year-old daughter. Even though I had never been married and had no children, I had my own parenting philosophy. On one occasion before our marriage, his daughter committed what I considered a "spankable" offense, and I was curious to see how Jim would respond. When he gave her an appropriately placed swat, I knew we could work in unity on this parenting thing! After we married, he told his daughter, in my presence, that he expected her to obey me even as she obeyed him, and I had his authority to discipline her in his absence.

In addition, he let me know our marriage came first. He knew that keeping our marriage strong was not only important for us as a couple but also the best thing he could do as a father. Jim's faith in me to partner with him in parenting gave me the confidence to take on the roles of both wife and instant mother. He neither dumped his parenting responsibilities on me nor undercut my authority. We are a team, partners in marriage and partners in parenting.

We have since added two more beautiful daughters to our family. Jim has continued to model a mixture of tenderness and firmness, as well as the mercy and justice of God in his role as their father. Seeing him parent his daughters with compassion and grace, while not "leaving the guilty unpunished," has only made me love him more.

Carol

Isn't that true—we are all parenting experts until we have kids. I love the deference that Carol showed to her husband. In so many instances, a woman can assume she is the parenting expert. I'll never forget when my friend Sonja was telling her husband all the things he was doing "wrong" (i.e., differently than she would have done them) with their new baby. Mitchell stopped, looked at her, and said, "As far as I know, we became parents at the same time, didn't we?"

The LORD, the LORD, the compassionate and gracious God, slow to anger, abounding in love and faithfulness, maintaining love to thousands, and forgiving wickedness, rebellion and sin. Yet he does not leave the guilty unpunished. (Exod. 34:6–7)

I thank you, Father, for the way you treat us and show us how a father loves his children. I ask you to produce these same characteristics in my husband's heart so that his love reflects and resembles yours. Let him see our children as a rich blessing and a gift from your hand. May our children see you in him and learn more about you by the way he models your love and character. Give him compassion and grace toward our children. Let him be slow to anger. Help him to abound in unconditional love for them, and grant him faithfulness in his fatherly responsibilities to protect them, provide for them, and guide them. May he make his children a high priority.

Keep my husband's love for his children healthy, strong, and enduring. Grant him your supernatural ability to forgive all of their wickedness, rebellion, and sin. Father, when they are young, teach him how to recognize the difference between childish irresponsibility and willful defiance and to know the appropriate means of discipline. As they grow, help him to be neither too strict nor too lenient, and always to take appropriate action. Give him courage to make unpopular decisions and strength to maintain consistency in his words and actions. May he make the necessary transitions in his parenting as our children mature into adulthood.

Increase his faith in you to guide him even as he guides our children, and give him confidence in his ability to be a good father. May our shared experience as parents strengthen our marriage.

I know I ask a lot, Lord, but parenting is an enormous job, and we need your wisdom, patience, and grace every step of the way. And now I need to ask one more thing of you—let your glory and the children's goodness be my husband's primary motivation in parenting. May he find great joy in his children and in his role as their father, even as you take joy in us.

Listen, my son, accept what I say,
    and the years of your life will be many.
I instruct you in the way of wisdom
    and lead you along straight paths. (Prov. 4:10–11)

I realize, Lord, as we turn our ears to your words, stay focused on you, and obey what is spoken in your Word, that we will flourish as we grow in Christ as husband and wife. May you expand our days together as we live with you at the center of our relationship. We ask, dear Lord, that you will pour out your wisdom upon us and keep us on the straight path as we head through this journey with you. Keep our eyes gazing forever in your direction, that we might not lose sight of the promises waiting for us.

My son, pay attention to what I say;
    turn your ear to my words.
Do not let them out of your sight,
    keep them within your heart;
for they are life to those who find them
    and health to one's whole body. (Prov. 4:20–22)

I'm praying that my husband will take heed of your Word and never allow your truth to escape him. Help him to bind it to his heart and mind so he will be able to lead his family down the path of righteousness. By doing so, he will find rest and peace within himself, which in turn will extend to his family. Make him aware of when he isn't listening to you. Help him to hear you and to have the desire to be obedient to the things of God.

Fathers, do not exasperate your children; instead, bring them up in the training and instruction of the Lord. (Eph. 6:4)

I see many children becoming angry and upset by the way their father deals with them. Dear Lord, I pray that my husband will not aggravate or make our children angry but will teach them your gentleness and love. May they be productive individuals because of that love. There is so much bad parenting in the world today, and as a result, there are many angry people. I pray that as we nurture and love our children as you tell us to, we will reap the results in future generations. Thank you, Lord, for your Word to guide us.

But the fruit of the Spirit is love, joy, peace, forbearance, kindness, goodness, faithfulness. (Gal. 5:22)

I realize, Lord, that we all have strengths and weaknesses in our character. In faith I come to you today to lift up my husband in prayer, asking you to give him the ability to be strong and courageous without reservation. I pray that you will equip him with the fruit of the Spirit and help him to have balance in his life. Teach him to be consistent so that he will bear the fruit of the Spirit and walk in your path of righteousness.

Whoever spares the rod hates their children,
but the one who loves their children is careful to discipline them. (Prov. 13:24)

Help us, Lord, to discipline our children the way you say we need to. We need your help to learn the best ways to discipline and not become lenient. Help us to teach our kids the way they need to go and how to live.

And do not grumble, as some of them did—and were killed by the destroying angel.

These things happened to them as examples and were written down as warnings for us, on whom the culmination of the ages has come. So, if you think you are standing firm, be careful that you don't fall! No temptation has overtaken you except what is common to mankind. And God is faithful; he will not let you be tempted beyond what you can bear. But when you are tempted, he will also provide a way out so that you can endure it. (1 Cor. 10:10–13)

I know, Lord, that to grumble is a sin, and we have made it more of an acceptable sin. But then, what is an "acceptable" sin in your eyes? I believe there is none. Therefore, help both my husband and myself to stop our grumbling and complaining about our children. Help us not to fall into the temptation to complain. Remind us daily of this sin, and help us to look for your path to get us through this trial. You will not bring a situation into our lives that you will not provide a way out of, and you will help us along the way.

Here is another way to pray this Scripture:

Help us not to grumble, as some of the Israelites did—and were killed by the destroying angel. These things happened to them as examples and were written down as warnings for us, on whom the culmination of the ages has come. So, if we think we're standing firm, help us to be careful that we don't fall! No temptation has overtaken us except what is common to mankind. And you are faithful; you will not let us be tempted beyond what we can bear. But when we are tempted, you will also provide a way out so that we can endure it.

Do everything without grumbling or arguing, so that you may become blameless and pure, "children of God without fault in a warped and crooked generation." Then you will shine among them like stars in the sky. (Phil. 2:14–15)

I pray that my husband will never get tired of doing well. I don't want to demand my way and set my husband up for failure. I ask, Lord, that you will teach my husband to pray when he is tempted to grumble or complain. We live in a wicked generation, and there are many ways my husband can be pulled onto unwanted paths that lead to destruction. My prayer for him today is that he will remain strong in Christ Jesus. May he be found blameless and pure and shine among all people.

18

His Mind

The prayer closet is the arena which produces the overcomer.

Paul E. Billheimer

There is a battle going on for our husbands' minds. Whether it's while watching TV, through interactions at work, or even in the messages they receive from church, our husbands' minds are under attack throughout the week.

I'm on the message team at our church. Once a week I get together with four of the pastors to brainstorm ideas about the topics and Scripture that our lead pastor, Scott, will be teaching on. During one discussion, we were talking about the upcoming messages for Mother's Day and Father's Day. As we were looking at some of the common themes that are preached on those days, Scott pointed out, "Have you ever noticed that every Mother's Day, churches give out roses and boxes of candy and tell moms how great they are, and then on Father's Day they spend the entire service telling dads that they need to do better by their wives and kids?" I had never noticed it before, but he was right. Our guys didn't need to go outside the church to get beat up. It was happening right there on Sunday morning.

Our prayers on our husbands' behalf are critical so they can avoid getting twisted in Satan's lies.

I love how speaker Emily Nelson describes a man's battle of the mind:

> The world's lies are really Satan's lies disguised as social acceptance: "Climb the corporate ladder! Just do it! Go for the gusto! If it feels good, do it! The more, the better!" Our men want to be at the top of their game, powerful, virile. When business is down or they lose their job, their worth crashes with it. When they age, they think it's all downhill, that they are withered and impotent.
>
> This is what my husband, Gregg, goes through. He says when he sees couples pushing strollers, he remembers those days with such hope and excitement, just cresting on success, with so much to look forward to. Now, at fifty-seven, he feels like the best has already happened. That depresses me, so I tell him to look on the positive side—we are wiser, have more time to ourselves, and are more settled financially. He still wants to be young with a full head of hair! And instead of me talking him out of his funk, he wants me to resonate with what he's saying. He wants me to hear his longing and say, "That's okay. I still love you and I'm in it with you!" When I try to snap him out of it, he feels I don't understand him. I need to validate his feelings, let him get his arms around this transition (we are recent empty nesters), and most of all pray that God grows something beautiful out of this time. Here is my prayer, based on Romans 12:2:
>
> *Lord, the world is beckoning my husband with its bright lights like a Vegas strip. But its promises are as fruitless as a slot machine. Lord, may he not put his quarters into empty*

promises. May he not be conformed to this world but be transformed by your truth and the renewing of his mind, that he may prove what is the good, acceptable, and perfect will of God. Lord, you know his anxiousness about growing older and becoming less effective, but I pray he will be worried about none of that, and that he may continually bring everything to you in prayer, with thanksgiving, for whatever stage of life he is in. May he pour out his heart to you, the one who listens with sympathetic, understanding ears.

Praying God's Word for His Thoughts

Do not be anxious about anything, but in every situation, by prayer and petition, with thanksgiving, present your requests to God. And the peace of God, which transcends all understanding, will guard your hearts and your minds in Christ Jesus. (Phil. 4:6–7)

May your peace surround his mind, peace that the world's philosophies don't provide—a peace that passes all understanding. May he know that your peace will guard his heart and mind because of his relationship with you, Jesus.

So I tell you this, and insist on it in the Lord, that you must no longer live as the Gentiles do, in the futility of their thinking. They are darkened in their understanding and separated from the life of God because of the ignorance that is in them due to the hardening of their hearts. (Eph. 4:17–18)

Lord, I thank you that my husband is a man of faith. He does not follow the futility of the world's thinking but is joined to life in you by your gift of salvation. Give light to his mind and help him to understand your ways.

We demolish arguments and every pretension that sets itself up against the knowledge of God, and we take captive every thought to make it obedient to Christ. (2 Cor. 10:5)

May he bring every thought captive to your obedience.

Finally, brothers and sisters, whatever is true, whatever is noble, whatever is right, whatever is pure, whatever is lovely, whatever is admirable—if anything is excellent or praiseworthy—think about such things. (Phil. 4:8)

Lord, for every thought that enters the door to his mind, I pray that he would filter it using your truth. Is this thought true? Is it noble? Is it right and pure? Is it lovely and admirable? Is it praiseworthy? If not, then kick it out! Do not let it cross the threshold of his mind. Guard his mind, Lord. May he meditate only on your truth.

Drink water from your own cistern,
running water from your own well.
Should your springs overflow in the streets,
your streams of water in the public squares?
Let them be yours alone,
never to be shared with strangers. (Prov. 5:15–17)

I pray that my husband will intentionally protect his eyes and heart from the sensual temptations of our culture. His heart is good and godly, but he is a man, and like all men, he is turned on by things he sees. I pray that no matter what he sees, he will always come home to me, and as Proverbs says, he will always desire to drink water from his own cistern. And I pray that I will always be a ready cistern!

Your statutes are wonderful;
therefore I obey them.
The unfolding of your words gives light;
it gives understanding to the simple.
I open my mouth and pant,
longing for your commands.
Turn to me and have mercy on me,
as you always do to those who love your name.
Direct my footsteps according to your word;
let no sin rule over me.
Redeem me from human oppression,
that I may obey your precepts.

Make your face shine on your servant
    and teach me your decrees.
Streams of tears flow from my eyes,
    for your law is not obeyed. (Ps. 119:129–36)

Lord, the testimony of how you have changed lives is wonderful. Allow those stories of how your marvelous light now rules where death once reigned to penetrate the heart of my husband. As your Word flows into him, unfold your light and grant him understanding. I know he longs for you, but the enemy has a strong pull on him. As he thirsts and hungers for you, protect him from the enemy's snare. Be gracious to him and establish his footsteps in your Word. Do not allow iniquity to hold him, but redeem him from the oppression of this world. Shine your face upon him and teach him your truth. Revive him, O Lord.

The end of all things is near. Therefore be alert and of sober mind so that you may pray. Above all, love each other deeply, because love covers over a multitude of sins. (1 Pet. 4:7–8)

I pray for my husband to be clear-minded and self-controlled. Remind him to pray, and help him to love others as you do. Help him to forgive others just as you have forgiven him.

Finally, brothers and sisters, rejoice! Strive for full restoration, encourage one another, be of one mind, live in peace. And the God of love and peace will be with you. (2 Cor. 13:11)

Help my husband and me to be one-minded and to live in peace. Help both of us to strive harder for restoration. Thank you, dear Lord, for your unfailing and ever-faithful love and peace.

I appeal to you, brothers and sisters, in the name of our Lord Jesus Christ, that all of you agree with one another in what you say and that there be no divisions among you, but that you be perfectly united in mind and thought. (1 Cor. 1:10)

I pray, dear Lord, for you to help my husband to be more agreeable not only toward us, his family, but also toward others around him. I pray there will be no divisions among us or among the people he works with.

Therefore let us stop passing judgment on one another. Instead, make up your mind not to put any stumbling block or obstacle in the way of a brother or sister. (Rom. 14:13)

I pray that you will help my husband not to pass judgment on others. Remind him often that he is to be salt and light to others. Remove any preconceived ideas that can be stumbling blocks or obstacles to others. Help me also to follow these words.

Therefore everyone who hears these words of mine and puts them into practice is like a wise man who built his house on the rock. (Matt. 7:24)

May my husband's thoughts always rest on your firm foundation. When worldly ideas enter his mind, let him hear the wise words of Jesus and stand on the rock of his salvation. Help him to think and reflect before he speaks or acts in ways not pleasing to you. Forgive him when his mind wanders on shifting sands. Redeem his thoughts, dear Lord, and place his focus on your love and grace.

Conclusion

Intercession is the most unselfish thing anyone
can do.

Paul E. Billheimer

I started this prayer adventure because I wanted to support
Roger. I wanted to see God move in my husband's life in new
and exciting ways. I wanted Roger to know that I've got his
back, both when life is good and when it's hard. And while
I've been praying for change in my husband's life, I have felt
a not-so-subtle change in my own.

As I've prayed for Roger over the big and the small, the
possible and the impossible, my trust in the One I'm praying
to has grown.

I used to feel unsure of myself—as if I wasn't quite qualified
to pray. That I wasn't intimate enough with God to be asking
for so much. But I love what Richard Foster says about the way
we come to our Father: "In the same way that a small child
cannot draw a bad picture so a child of God cannot offer a
bad prayer."[3] God has proven himself to me over and over. He
is listening, and he cares for my husband even more than I do.

There was a period of time recently when Roger was feeling overcome in a situation in ministry. We both knew that the problem wasn't going to change, and either Roger was going to have to accept the undesirable situation, or he was going to have to step down from his role. We didn't feel confirmation for either step—we just felt stuck.

I started to pray for the impossible situation based on John 16:33: "These things I have spoken to you, so that in Me you may have peace. In the world you have tribulation, but take courage; I have overcome the world" (NASB). I prayed, *God, Roger is lacking peace about this ministry. He doesn't have peace about staying or leaving. Father, I pray that Roger will live out his trust in you during this situation. We know that you can overcome anything. We put our trust in you.*

In just the next couple of months, God miraculously moved the pieces of that ministry around, bringing in new leadership and putting procedures into place. What seemed impossible just a few months before was now completed.

I know it's easy to read about someone else's situation in a book and think, *Great, that worked for her, but my situation is different; my husband is different.* I understand. But I also know that we have a God who is in the business of showing up and showing off.

I pray that someday I will get to hear the story of what God has done in your husband's life—and in yours.

Notes

1. A. J. Gossip, *The Galilean Accent* (Edinburgh: T & T Clark, 1926), 75.

2. Cindi McMenamin, *When a Woman Inspires Her Husband* (Eugene, OR: Harvest House Publishers, 2011), 110.

3. Richard Foster, *Prayer: Finding the Heart's True Home* (New York: HarperOne, 1992), 8–9.

Scripture Index

Kathi Lipp is the author of *The Husband Project*, *The Marriage Project*, *The Me Project*, and *The "What's for Dinner?" Solution*. Kathi's articles have appeared in dozens of magazines, and she is a frequent guest on Focus on the Family radio and TV. She and her husband, Roger, are the parents of four teens and young adults in San Jose, California. Kathi shares her story at retreats, conferences, and women's events across the United States. Connect with her at www.KathiLipp.com.

Thanks for reading *Praying God's Word for Your Husband*. I'm grateful, and I know your husband and your marriage will be blessed!

One of my favorite things in the world is to hear from the women who've read my books. I would love to stay in touch.

· · ·

Visit
WWW.KATHILIPP.COM
to join with other women who are praying for their husbands.

And if you're leading a group through *Praying God's Word for Your Husband,* be sure to check out the "For Leaders" section.

Other ways to reach me:

info@kathilipp.com
kathilipp.author
kathilipp

Kathi Lipp
171 Branham Lane
Suite 10-122
San Jose, CA 95136

Inspirational Devotions for Mom

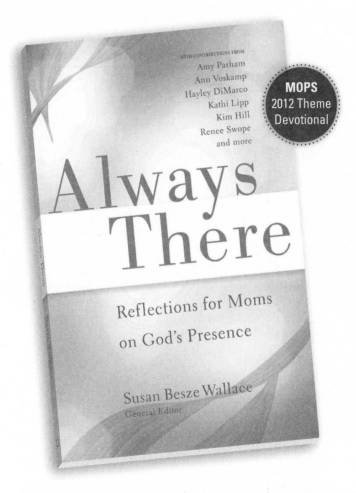

A devotional for moms by moms, using real-life
mothering stories and Scripture to illustrate God's
abiding presence in their lives.

Revell
a division of Baker Publishing Group
www.RevellBooks.com

Available wherever books are sold.

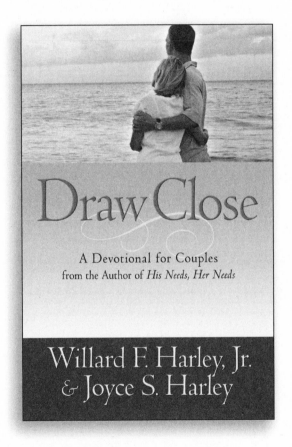